Praise for *Brand Against the Machine*

"John is a rebellious leader of a new form of branding. He doesn't pull any punches and delivers straightforward advice you can't afford to ignore."

—**Barry Moltz**, author of *Bounce!*

"As a business owner, it's easy to get lost in the crowds and noise, which is why a powerful brand is crucial. Other so-called brand experts seem to be riding a trend of what business owners see as the next miracle cure. But John Morgan is different. Branding is a lifestyle, a signature, and, quite simply, what he breathes on a cellular level. Don't waste your time studying branding with anyone else. Just read, listen, and watch John. I know I do."

—**Carrie Wilkerson**, author of *The Barefoot Executive*

"This ain't your mother's world of branding anymore. *Brand Against the Machine* is a punk rock look into the world of branding. This book will help you get ahead of the crowd by surfing right over it and jumping right into the mosh pit of business."

—**Amber Osborne**, aka Miss Destructo

"*Brand Against the Machine* is a wake-up call for business owners with its ruthless challenging of assumptions about branding and marketing. If you want to build a business that not only gets noticed, but also gets cared about, then read this book today."

—**Dr. Mollie Marti**, author of *The 12 Factors of Business Success*

"John nailed it with this one sentence from the book: 'The future of branding is marketing WITH people and not AT them.' This book is filled with real wisdom from a super smart marketer and is one that every business owner should read immediately."

—**Ryan Lee**, author, entrepreneur, coach, speaker

"There are thousands of people you can turn to for branding. But there's only *one* who has the creativity, chops, and spot-on insight to help you perfectly connect to your market—John Morgan. *Brand Against the Machine* is your invitation to step out of the shadows and move from invisible to unavoidable."

—**Paul Evans**, author and speaker

"John Morgan will definitely change the way you think about branding and marketing your business. John is one of the smartest branding experts around. His strategies are second to none. You owe it to yourself and to your customers to listen. Read *Brand Against the Machine* today!"

—**Kristi Frank**, celebrity, diet guru, and former star of *The Apprentice* with Donald Trump

"Branding is one of those topics businesspeople throw around in conversation but don't truly understand. If you've ever been secretly confused about what personal branding is or simply want to know exactly how to create and communicate your own powerful brand so that you are in demand, you've got to read this book. John Morgan's no-nonsense style had me laughing out loud while taking notes from beginning to end."

—**Felicia J. Slattery**, author of *Cash In on Communication* and *Cinderella Interrupted*

"John has laser vision when it comes to brand development. John's genius lies in his ability to identify brand hooks that are remarkable and memorable. I have always been amazed at John's ability to see branding opportunities that increase his client's bottom line without fail. John is a student and teacher of great branding. His ability to leverage brand equity and pinpoint opportunities has helped his clients increase their bottom lines exponentially."

—**Perry Lawrence**, Mr. Video at AskMrVideo.com

"John Morgan is a leading authority on branding. John's depth of knowledge and practical takeaways are both compelling and exciting. You can take action immediately on John's advice. He explains things in a way that is relatable but at the same time takes everyone listening to a higher level of understanding. He's my go-to guy on all things branding."

—**Erin Blaskie**, www.erinblaskie.com

"If you think your brand isn't important, you need to hit yourself with a wet noodle and then crack open this book. John's words will break you down, stir you up, and then help you be able to *Brand Against the Machine*."

—**Jason Dykstra**, Absolution Mediation

"John Morgan is absolutely one of the most genuine, spot-on branding strategists I have had the pleasure of working with. He knows how to simply turn a person or a company into living a brand that speaks their message clearly and authentically, all while having fun and enjoying the ride. John has a unique ability to create a brand with you that feels unique, is completely you, and brings you the clients you can't wait to serve!"

—**Maruxa Murphy**, marketing and business coach

"John Morgan is a branding powerhouse. He has a knack for cutting through the noise to get a brand to *burst* into the marketplace. I can't count how many thousands of dollars he's saved me with sage advice and, more important, the thousands of dollars his advice has made me!"

—**Spencer Shaw**, serial entrepreneur

"Branding is one of those things that if it's done wrong, it can kill your business before it even gets off the ground, *but* if you do it the right way, the way John teaches, you can multiply your customer base, resonate more deeply with those customers, and have the successful business you envision."

—**Kyle Battis**, Internet entrepreneur

"John Morgan has forgotten more about business branding than most have ever known. Don't miss the opportunity to learn from him. He has the unique ability to deliver and teach branding in a fun and entertaining way."

—**Josh Hinds**, founder of GetMotivation.com

"When John Morgan speaks, I listen intently. If your goal is to build a lasting and powerful brand, this book will teach you how to navigate the murky waters of branding. Few people understand what makes a brand successful. John not only understands what others don't, but he also shares actionable strategies that will have an immediate impact on your business. I know this because I've seen it firsthand in my own company."

—**Travis Robertson**, peak performance coach and entrepreneur; owner of Don't Settle Media

"John Morgan's branding strategies and advice are both incredibly powerful and yet infinitely practical. Before I started working with John, I knew who I wanted to connect with, but I didn't know how to position myself and my services in a way that stood out and attracted my ideal clients to me. After John's coaching, I knew specifically who I was targeting, how to reach them, what to say to them, and how to position myself as the perfect person to serve their needs. John is the most honest, nonsalesy, clever, and down-to-earth branding expert I have ever met, and working with him was one of the best investments I have made in my consulting business."

—**Kendra D. Brodin**, legal career and professional development consultant

"John Morgan is called the 'Chuck Norris of Branding' for a reason—he gives brands glistening biceps. Get ready for the gun show by reading this book, or take warning that your brand might go missing in action."

—**Janet Wallace**, owner of Social Deviants

"John Morgan is not only an authority on branding, but also a genius at helping you discover your own unique voice. He is masterful at establishing credibility and adding fun to your marketing efforts. Without a doubt, John is an expert at helping entrepreneurs breathe life into their brands and their businesses. Every time I have contact with John, I never fail to be impressed at his marketing acumen and savvy."

—**Danielle Miller**, coach, DanielleMiller.com

"*Brand Against the Machine* is to business books what film was to the movie industry. Everything before now seems trite and out of place. John has written a book that will not only change how you see your business; it will change how you see yourself. If you don't read this book, you'd better start watching your back from those that have."

—**Joey Strawn**, social media strategist

"John Morgan will push your boundaries. With John's strategies I have gone from an unemployed website salesman to a business thought leader in my niche. John has helped shape the way I look at business."

—**Jason Elkins**, Transparent Media

"John is one of those rare people who proves what he preaches. His critical insights on branding aren't for everyone. But those who want their business to thrive can't afford to miss him."

—**Joel Widmer**, Fluxe Digital Marketing

"John Morgan is a cup of pure awesomeness. He's got more branding know-how in his pinkie than most agencies have in their entire team. His ideas and recommendations are a great combination of wisdom, humor, and heart. Your business will be wildly impacted by implementing his suggestions and strategies. I know mine has been!"

—**Mitch Matthews**, founder of The Big Dream Gathering

"Building my personal brand has been one of the most, if not *the* most, important business decisions I've ever made. As a result of the strategies I've learned from my good friend John, I've been positioned by every major media outlet in my local area as the go-to expert in my market. Now I've got a platform where I can make a huge impact in my local city and give back."

—**Alejandro Reyes**, blogger and speaker

"Swiping a Morgan-ism: if visibility gets you in the door and credibility keeps you there—John is well and truly cemented inside the house of personal branding."

—**James Reynolds**, Incredible Inc.

"John takes marketing know-how, trims off all the fat, and serves it up to you in easy-to-follow bite-sized pieces. This book is not only for the novice but also for the pro who has become overloaded with too much noise!"

—**Danny Griffin**, real estate coach

BRANDAGAINST THE MACHINE

How to Build Your Brand, Cut Through the Marketing Noise, and Stand Out from the Competition

JOHN MORGAN

WILEY

John Wiley & Sons, Inc.

Published by John Wiley & Sons, Inc., Hoboken, New Jersey.
Published simultaneously in Canada.

For general information on our other products and services or for technical support, please contact our Customer Care Department within the United States at (800) 762-2974, outside the United States at (317) 572-3993 or fax (317) 572-4002.

Wiley publishes in a variety of print and electronic formats and by print-on-demand. Some material included with standard print versions of this book may not be included in ebooks or in print-on-demand. If this book refers to media such as a CD or DVD that is not included in the version you purchased, you may download this material at http://booksupport.wiley.com. For more information about Wiley products, visit www.wiley.com.

Library of Congress Cataloging-in-Publication Data:

Morgan, John, 1961-
Brand against the machine : How to Build Your Brand, Cut Through the Marketing Noise, and Stand Out from the Competition
    p. cm.
  Includes index.
   ISBN 978-1-118-10352-4 (cloth); ISBN 978-1-118-16035-0 (ebk);
   ISBN 978-1-118-16034-3 (ebk); ISBN 978-1-118-16033-6
1. Branding (Marketing)   I. Title.
  HF5415.1255.M67 2012
  658.8'27–dc23

                                                                2011024074

Printed in the United States of America

10 9 8 7 6 5 4 3 2 1

To my amazing wife Brooke, for seeing something in me years before I saw it myself.

Contents

1

The Machine

IT WAS JANUARY 20, 1759, when English author Samuel Johnson said in his magazine *The Idler*, "Advertisements are now so numerous that they are very negligently perused, and it is therefore become necessary to gain attention by magnificence of promises, and by eloquence sometimes sublime and sometimes pathetic."

That was 252 years ago. Nothing has changed.

Every day we are hammered with thousands of messages that are pushed on us by brands regardless of whether or not we want them. Interrupting people over and over with your marketing message is the craziest way to do business I know. Yet every day, it's like a machine is producing message after message and shoving them down people's throats, hoping they will buy. This is the machine you and I are setting out to destroy.

People are bored to death about the way brands market themselves. The machine is producing sales pitch after sales pitch at an exhausting rate. People's attention spans are getting shorter by the day. Marketing isn't getting any easier.

It's time for change. The old ways of branding are ineffective. Are you ready to make a shift and stand out against the machine that pumps out crap day in and day out?

> The future of branding is marketing *with* people and not *at* them.

Today's marketplace is overcrowded and noisy. There's no shortage of competition. The good news is that despite an overcrowded marketplace, it's easier than ever to be unique. The Internet has provided us with so many tools and resources that allow us to build real relationships with our target audience. The relationship you have with your audience is critical to your brand's success.

Branding has hundreds of definitions. Your brand is simply the emotional connect people have with you or your business. Branding is about relationships, perception, positioning, and I could go on. Your brand lets people know who you are. It answers these questions: Who are you? What do you do? Who do you do it for?

> Branding isn't about market share, it's about mindshare.

Your goal is to position your brand in the mind of the consumer as one of, if not *the*, top authority in your industry, to be seen as a valued resource rather than another service provider. Advertising legend David Ogilvy once said, "Any damn fool can put on a deal, but it takes genius, faith, and perseverance to create a brand."

You have to know how to promote your brand and position it as something different than the competition. That's what this book is all about. I'm giving you the strategies you need to get your brand noticed and to build a community of raving fans.

You can become a highly successful personal brand in any field or industry. The sky is the limit. Personal brands are increasing the value of businesses dramatically. Think of a few of the world's most successful personal brands such as Oprah, Richard Branson, Martha Stewart, or Steve Jobs, and you can see the impact their brand has on their business.

It's often the case that people don't believe they can be a brand. The reality is you already have a personal brand because people already have a perception of you. Everyone who has ever met you has an opinion about you. Imagine if Charlie Sheen quit show business to start a babysitting business. Would you let him keep your kid? I hope not. You have a perception of him. In branding, as with many things, perception is reality.

You have to be prepared and equipped to harness the power of personal branding or prepare to become obsolete. Even if you are an employee (not an entrepreneur or business owner), you have tons of competition. The world is full of talented people ready to take your job or promotion. Your personal brand can be used for job promotions, and it should be used to help promote the company you work for.

You're about to discover many insights and strategies that are easy to implement and will increase your brand's presence and attract the right customers. This book is your guide on what to do and how to do it when it comes to increasing your presence and dominating your niche.

To brand against the machine is to create a reputation as a leading authority who provides value to people rather than being another "me too" business that blasts marketing messages at those who do not want them.

This isn't a book full of fluff or filler. It's to the point and rapid-fire. It's full of useful ideas, tips on executing those ideas, and the occasional example thrown in for good measure. This isn't a book about laws and rules. I hate rules. It's a book about what works. Do you have to do everything? Nope. But take what you can implement today and put it into action. You can always come back later and implement the rest.

This book isn't about using the newest thingamajig or tactic. It's about implementing strategies to build a sustainable brand and a business that serves you. It will give you a lot to think about. But I don't want it to stop there. It is full of things to do. My advice is to do them.

We don't have time to mess around.

If you've already got a brand and would like to strengthen it, you're in the right place. If you have a business but your brand isn't well known yet, you're in the right place.

The world we live in is extremely cluttered and even chaotic. The business world is no exception. People have developed a pattern of effort to ignore all marketing methods. You must work hard to build a brand that stands out and goes against the grain.

> Your brand is not a campaign. It's a commitment.

People embrace those who challenge the status quo. Those who win brand themselves against the tiresome mundane noise. They are the new leaders, a new form of brand that unites people and makes a difference.

Let's make a ruckus.

2

Why Branding?

I'M NOT GOING TO LECTURE you on all of the reasons why you should focus on branding. After all, you've already bought the book, so you must know there's some benefit to be had. That is, unless you're reading this in the bookstore, in which case you should immediately run to the register and buy it. Owning this book will instantly make you 27 percent more awesome. You want to be more awesome, don't you?

The terms *personal branding* and *branding* have become buzzwords. A lot of people are missing the key benefits of building a strong brand. The number one asset in your business is your brand. It's not your database or your price. It's not your product or your location. It's you.

> You are your biggest advantage.

What you do may not be unique, but you are. This is why putting your personality into your brand is so important. You're not in a niche or industry that is without competition. The only difference between you and your competition is your brand. Sure, your price may be lower, but how long will that last? Your product may have a benefit that your

5

competition doesn't offer. How long will that last? At some point your competition will match you. The one element they cannot match is your brand. There are a lot of businesses that make shoes. There is only one Nike.

> It's important you realize that *you*, not your product, create the value.

When my accountant does a good job I say, "Karl did an awesome job." I don't say, "CPA Services (or whatever his business name is) really did good." Your customers are the same. You're the one creating and providing the value. Your product or service is the avenue you used to provide that value.

If after reading this book you're thinking, "Wow! I now know how to get my brand to dominate my industry!" then you got the value from me. The book was just the tool used to deliver the message. And if you are thinking that, send me a note. My mom likes to put those on her fridge.

Having a strong brand beats the heck out of selling. Do you think once Oprah's brand was established she had to go around convincing people to be a guest on her show? Brands that are well positioned in the marketplace have less selling to do. They have a relationship with their target audience and a high level of trust with them as well. You begin to attract prospects rather than spending all of your time searching for them.

Brands can make people pay more for one thing than another similar thing. Branding is what makes me drive past a Kmart while going to Target. They sell the same stuff, for the most part. But I have a different perception of each of them. My trust level is different for each of them. Women and some strange dudes buy Coach Purses because of the emotional association with that brand. Could they buy a similar purse much cheaper? Yep, but it wouldn't be a Coach; therefore, in their mind it wouldn't be as good.

> Branding is about emotion, and emotion turns prospects into buyers.

People are willing to spend more money on a brand they trust. Do I want to drink a nice cold Kountry Mist or a Mountain Dew? Kountry Mist is a generic brand of Mountain Dew, and I have zero trust in that brand. Just because it's cheaper doesn't mean I'm gonna have a sip. Plus, it's annoying when brands get too cute with the spelling of their name. Spelling country with a K makes me worry about their education. It isn't kool.

People also stick around longer with brands they trust. They are more likely to become customers for life. One of the reasons they stick around longer is that they are more forgiving of your mistakes. Amazon.com is a phenomenal brand; however, like any brand, it isn't perfect. When someone began selling a book on Amazon that was targeted at pedophiles, people were in an uproar, and rightfully so. After getting hit with bad publicity and getting an earful from the social media world, Amazon removed the book. Their brand suffered a black eye, but today no one has an issue purchasing from Amazon. People are forgiving of mistakes, especially when they have a good relationship with the brand.

Another wonderful benefit of branding is that people buy more from you. Tom Hanks is one of the greatest actors of all time. His fans will watch any movie he's in regardless of what the movie is about. They trust him, and they are familiar with him. Heck, I even sat through the movie *The Ladykillers* just because Tom was in it.

Branding works in any market, big or small. Home Depot and Lowe's are the two big brands in the home improvement space. Although they are large brands doing very well, there are still several small home improvement stores in my town that are also doing well. Their market is small and their brand is small. Yet they have a great reputation and relationship with their audience.

A strong brand gives prospects a comfort level so they actually prequalify themselves. They respect you and know if they are a fit with your brand. For example, you don't just run out and test-drive a Ferrari for the heck of it. You only shop for a Ferrari when you know you are financially able to and, most likely, after you've done a lot of research on the car. You're a fan of Ferrari before you buy it. Because of Ferrari's position in the marketplace, the salespeople aren't dealing with tire kickers. They are dealing with prospects who have a very real interest in purchasing a high-performance car.

> Want better clients? Build a better brand.

Even brands that are focused on mass-producing products can and do benefit from personal branding. It's still real people at the company creating those products and providing those services. It's easy to abandon a faceless brand. The corporate voice doesn't work well anymore.

Living in the South in the United States, we call every beverage Coke. If I order a Coke and the server asks, "Is Pepsi okay?" I say sure. Why? Because I have no emotional attachment to the brand because I have no relationship with anyone there. I don't feel connected to them. People connect with people, not a product or faceless brand.

There is no gap between traditional corporate branding and personal branding. Personal brands can coexist with a company brand. Take Scott Monty, for example. Scott is the head of social media at the Ford Motor Company. Ford is doing a good job of letting us know the people behind the logo. Scott is building relationships with people and is a brand within a brand.

Richard Branson is the founder of Virgin, one of the world's largest brands. He is perhaps the most visible and well-known personal brand within a larger brand. Richard has allowed us to get to know him and his dreams for the world. Because of the fondness we have for him, we have a fondness for Virgin as well.

The Ultimate Fighting Championship, or UFC, really understands how personal brands can connect with their fans. They are encouraging their fighters to tweet as much as possible. Dana White, president of the UFC, is giving them incentives for doing so. They understand that personal brands from their fighters reinforce the UFC brand overall. They are giving their fans a chance to connect and engage with their favorite fighters.

> Branding is not just about being seen as better than the competition. It's about being seen as the *only* solution to your audience's problem.

Your desired outcomes for your brand are to establish your personal brand as an authority in your field, showcase your credibility, and build real relationships and trust with your target audience. The world doesn't need another corporate brand. It needs *you*. We need your input, advice, message, and solutions.

Even if you own a large business with lots of employees, it's still real people promoting your product and real people buying it. People do business with people. They connect and engage with people. Corporate branding is no longer an effective strategy. Today people connect with your personality, content, and values. Not your product or service.

> You are your brand.

The longer you go without branding yourself, the more your competition will establish a relationship with your audience and win. Most entrepreneurs never take the time to think about their position in the marketplace or develop a plan of how they will promote themselves. You must be dedicated to your brand and what you stand for.

The big benefit of having a powerful brand is that you attract business rather than having to chase people down and beg for it. You position yourself in the marketplace so that they find you. The more well known you are, the more successful you will be. You want to be a name that people drop. When people are mentioning you in casual conversation, you know it's working.

Build a brand based on your goals. If you don't want to sell your business one day, then don't. Everyone asks, "What about when you want to sell?" The majority of people who ask that have never sold a business. Get it to the point where someone would want to buy it first. Then worry about selling it.

> Define yourself before someone else does.

Some branding experts will tell you to let your audience define you. That is a dangerous suggestion because they may put you in a box you do not want to be in. If I'm attending a networking event and someone asks what I do, my response is not "You tell me." It's on me to make it clear what my brand is about. From there the audience will decide if it's right for them. If you don't define it, they will, and they could screw it up.

Branding is fluid and constant. Branding isn't a logo or color scheme. It's not a one-time deal, either. Personal branding is extremely effective, and 99 percent of the strategies you can implement to build your brand are free.

Personal branding is about building a tribe of raving fans and putting your energy into creating value for them. As you do this, your fans will support you and buy from you.

Branding requires a great deal of patience. Oftentimes the benefits of branding are unseen, but that doesn't mean they go unnoticed. Your brand works for you or against you, but it always works.

3

The Brand Framework

FOR MOST PEOPLE, BRANDING IS AN AFTERTHOUGHT. They are so focused on creating products and marketing those products that they let branding happen naturally. The challenge they face is that by not having a solid branding strategy, they are left constantly trying to create that next product that will be a hit or the next marketing idea that will catch on and spread virally. That's a lot of pressure and stress that can be relieved by having a framework for your branding efforts.

Six steps within your branding framework will set you on the path to success. We cover each step in detail throughout the book, but here's a quick rundown for you to understand the big picture here.

The first step in your branding framework is to know your audience, which goes beyond just identifying target market. It's about knowing what your target market wants. You need to know what frustrates them the most. Your product or service will solve the problem that is frustrating them. You need to know what it is they want. Notice I said what they *want*, not need. When my son Jack *needs* to take a bath, he never *wants* to. People buy what they want, not what they need. You also need to know what they think it will take to solve their problem. If they already have an idea of what the solution may look like, you can be sure your product matches that idea.

11

The second step in this framework is to define your position. Branding is all about positioning. It's not about market share; it's about being thought of as the *only* choice in your field. Positioning yourself as the go-to authority in your industry is the goal. If you're a chiropractor, for example, you want to be the first person people think of when they need a back adjustment.

The third step is to create a solution. You know what's bugging your audience. Now it's time to make sure your product or service is a cure for what ails them. If what you sell isn't a solution to their problems, then you're not going to sell very much. Find a problem and create a solution has been the formula for entrepreneurial success for generations.

The fourth step in your branding framework is content. It is your content that will attract people to you and will assist in establishing your authority positioning. By producing high-quality content that your target audience finds valuable, you will attract prospects to you versus trying to track them down and sell to them the old-fashioned way by bombarding them with ad after ad begging them to buy. The key to effective branding is attracting people to you and then building a relationship with them through engagement with your audience. Attract first; then engage. You attract by offering them valuable information. The more you give, the more attractive your brand becomes.

The fifth step in your framework is promotion. This is where most brands get it wrong. Your ability to promote your brand and your products/services will determine how successful you are. Promotion isn't a one-time thing. You should always have a promotional campaign in motion. The difference between the promotions that the machine pumps out and you is that your campaigns will be content driven. You will be viewed as a welcome guest in their lives rather than an annoying pest.

The sixth and final step in your branding framework is to over-deliver your value. There is simply too much competition to produce a product or service that just delivers.

Fulfill your promises. If you imply that your product or service is great when in fact it's actually crap, then you are a liar.

When Steve Jobs announced the iPad, a lot of people didn't see a need for it in the marketplace. Steve told us it was awesome and that we would love it. If the iPad turned out to be a piece of junk, it surely wouldn't have found its place in the market. But Steve wasn't lying. The iPad *is* awesome.

Your product or service has to go above and beyond and give customers more value than they were expecting. As Walt Disney said, "Do what you do so well that they will want to see it again and bring their friends." Don't just strive to meet customers' expectations. Strive to exceed their expectations.

Many businesses have a very good product yet don't experience the type of success they are trying to achieve because they do not know how to effectively communicate their brand message to people. You must learn to communicate clearly. It doesn't matter how much value you offer or how good you are at what you do if you cannot communicate it to your audience.

> Prospects will never see the value in you if you cannot communicate it clearly to them.

Are you a relationship marketer or transaction marketer?

Marketing for the sake of generating a transaction will become increasingly difficult. Today and for the future, marketing is about relationships. Sales transactions become easy when an existing relationship is there.

Remember: The future of business is marketing *with* people, not *at* them.

4

Visibility versus Ability

CAN YOU THINK OF ONE OF YOUR COMPETITORS who is very successful even though they aren't nearly as experienced or skilled as you? The one that leaves you scratching your head about why they are on top and you are not? I'm going to tell you why, and I will reveal the harsh reality about branding and marketing and the truth about why inferior products and services often end up as the market leaders.

> Your visibility is more important than your ability.

When it comes to branding, size matters. The more visible you are, the more you win. It doesn't matter if you're more skilled or have more talent. The most visible brands are those who have opportunities come their way while invisible brands do not.

People get paid for who they are more than for what they do. We see this happen with celebrities every day. Paris Hilton doesn't get paid to attend events because she's a riveting conversationalist. She gets paid to attend events because of her name recognition. People don't always choose the most deserving person or company to work with. Business is a popularity contest.

14

Now, by no means am I saying that you can have a bad product or service as long as your brand is visible. That is a surefire way to make sure your brand is known for all of the wrong reasons. You will never get any repeat business or referrals if you can't deliver on the goods. You still have to have the ability.

> Visibility gets people in the door, *but* your ability keeps them there.

Most people fall into a trap that I call the *Field of Dreams* approach to marketing. They believe that if they build it, they will come. If you think this way, I've got terrible news for you. No one is coming for your product or service. No one is going out of their way to discover you. Just because you have a product to sell doesn't mean anyone will buy it.

You know the old saying, "Build a better mousetrap and the world will beat a path to your door?" It's only half true. It should read, "Build a better mousetrap and the world will beat a path to your door *if they know about it*."

You may have an incredible product or service, and I truly hope that you do. But having a great product or service isn't going to be enough. If no one knows you exist, the best product in the world isn't going to save you.

An overwhelming number of good products are on the market. However, just because a product is good doesn't mean it's worth talking about. Producing a good—or even a great product—doesn't mean people will come busting down your door to buy it.

> It's estimated that 1 to 5 percent of people who come in contact with your brand will become clients. Are you coming in contact with enough people?

If you're not going to create visibility for your brand, you had better hope you have a ginormous marketing budget to start buying people's attention. Pepsi can afford to blow money on Super Bowl ads. Most brands cannot, especially personal brands. If you do have this kind of budget, you are extremely fortunate and shouldn't be shocked that you make the rest of us sick.

Having a large marketing budget doesn't guarantee success. Most brands that have a large budget are by no means remarkable. There is nothing exciting or unique about what they do, which is one reason why they need a large marketing budget to push their message onto the marketplace. This creates a *huge* opportunity for you to brand against the machine and be a brand that is unique and worth talking about, a brand that people can really get behind.

Perception is reality. The more well known your brand, the more people want to be a part of it. If they've never heard of you, they won't be too impressed.

The more visible your brand, the more sales you make. Increased visibility equals increased credibility. People have more trust in a brand they are familiar with.

Visibility has changed branding. Scratch that. Visibility has killed traditional branding. Traditional branding didn't just change, it actually died, but there was no funeral for it and the world didn't care enough about it to make any arrests. In fact, a number of people may even have celebrated.

The idea that a brand's visibility is built with billboards and fancy logos no longer makes sense. Google is one of the largest brands in the world, and they have spent relatively little money on traditional "branding" methods such as advertising. They've spent so little on advertising, their logo looks like any kindergarten-age child with four crayons could have designed it.

Brands following that old-school approach are destined to fail. If you think your product being awesome is enough, you are destined to fail.

Keep in mind that you don't need to be found everywhere, as traditional branding would suggest. You just want to be found everywhere within your niche, everywhere your audience is hanging out.

Visibility is all about being consistent. You must be active and be "out there" every single day. You want to maintain your visibility and momentum. There's no time to slow down.

Now that you know the importance of focusing on visibility, we are going to dive into all of the ways to grow your brand into a powerhouse. A brand that people can relate to, trust, and talk about.

5

Attention Doesn't Equal Trust

FOR DECADES, BUSINESSES HAVE SHOVED their marketing message and sales offers in our faces. Every single day we're hit with thousands of marketing messages that are begging for our attention. In fact, it's estimated we see between 1,700 and 3,000 advertising messages per day. The system is broken. The majority of these ads are ignored. The few that actually get our attention are rarely, if ever, remembered.

Most people blast their marketing message out to the world hoping to interrupt and gain attention. This is what traditional branding is all about: Plaster your message on a billboard, run daily radio spots and TV commercials, and hope the right people notice it. I don't want to build my brand or business on hope. Do you?

Most people find this approach acceptable because they feel like they are increasing the awareness of their brand. But there is a major problem with that:

AWARENESS AND ATTENTION DO NOT EQUAL TRUST!

That's right; I just went all caps on you. Just because someone is aware of you or your product doesn't mean they trust you, and it sure as heck doesn't mean they want to do business with you. Awareness isn't the point.

In Chapter 4 I mentioned how visibility is more important than ability. But if a person being aware of you isn't enough, then how does visibility win out? It's about being known by your target audience. You don't want them to just be aware of you; you want them to like and trust you. You do that by focusing on them.

Your branding and marketing efforts must be focused on establishing and building trust with your audience. When someone trusts you, they are more welcoming and responsive to your marketing. You are seen as a welcome guest rather than an annoying pest.

When you're trying to get your message in front of everyone, you end up causing your target market to feel ignored. They want to know you're speaking directly to them.

In an effort to make all of my science teachers in school happy, I'm going to use light as an analogy. Trust me; it doesn't get any geekier than this. Light can only shine one of two ways. It can shine direct and focused like a laser. Or it can shine spread out like a light bulb.

Most marketing efforts are like a light bulb. They are spread out and trying to hit everyone at once. It needs to be more laser focused and directed toward your target audience.

Every piece of content you create and every single marketing message should be geared toward your target audience. It's not for the masses. All of those old high school buddies on Facebook who don't understand why you blog and talk about business, learn to ignore them. They aren't who you're after.

When your message is focused and directed toward a certain group of people, those people respond. They respond because they realize it's for them. That's the kind of attention you want. With the attention of the right people and by taking care of those people, you can start to build trust and a loyal audience.

Most people try to sell to anyone with a pulse. The world is full of billions of people. That's a lot of people to try to market to. But you aren't after billions. You're only trying to earn the attention of your slice of the population. You'll never be all things to everyone, so don't even try.

When you try to let your marketing message hit everyone, it becomes watered down and has little to no impact. You must focus on those that matter. The ones that matter are the people most likely to become a customer.

Focus on your audience, and ignore the rest.

Don't make the mistake of spending your time and energy on people who are not your target audience. I see this a *lot* in the wonderful world of social media. You know better than to assume the whole world wants your product or service. That type of unfocused blanket marketing is a recipe for disaster. Focus on your fans and focus on the people who will become fans.

The more time and energy you spend communicating with people who do not fit your target market, the more you alienate those who do. I have seen authors ignore every positive comment on Amazon about their book and then turn around and respond to every single negative comment they have received, even going so far as to offer them some one-on-one time on the phone. Really? Here's a tip: Take care of those who take care of you and forget the haters.

You can't focus on your target audience until you define them. Your target audience is the group of people most likely to purchase from you and those you are in the best position to serve. All of your marketing efforts should be directed at these people. Focus all of your attention on them. The rest are irrelevant.

Build a profile of what your ideal client looks like. What problems do they have that you can solve? Who are the people most likely to have those problems?

An easy way to do this is to take a look at your 10 favorite clients. And don't tell me they are all your favorites or I'll have to punch you in the kidneys. Look at those 10 and evaluate what made them your favorite. Were they respectful? Were they fun to work with? Did they pay a lot and pay on time?

The next step is to see what all these 10 clients have in common. Are the majority of them female? Are they all in the same age group? Do they live in the same geographic location? Finally, how did you serve them? What problems did they have that you solved?

The answers to these questions help you identify who that ideal client or customer is. Once you know, you can target all of your efforts toward them. Your marketing can focus on solving their problems and showing them that your brand is the perfect fit for them.

Most brands create a product or service and then go chasing after customers. This approach is completely backward. Picture your target clients, and then create a solution to their problems.

37 Signals is a software firm based out of Chicago. The team at 37 Signals approaches product creation differently than most. They build their products to solve their own problems. They scratch their own itch. They don't rush out and create product and then search for people to buy it. They see a problem they have and then create a solution. They are their target audience. It's safe for them to assume that if they have a problem, others like them probably do as well.

Because of this perspective, the team created a product called Basecamp, one of the most popular project management tools on the market. Additionally, 37 Signals offers other products that solve very specific needs for their audience.

Perhaps most fascinating is their willingness to refuse to add certain features to their products. They don't attempt to be all things to all people. The company has built up a reputation for rejecting most of the feature requests they receive so that they can stay true to their goal of providing an easy-to-use project management tool. This willingness to build only for their target customers has helped the company grow into an extremely profitable business.

If you take the time to define your ideal client, not only will you now know target customers when you see them, but they will know they've found who they are looking for. By speaking their language and addressing their needs, they know they've found a business they can trust.

Always keep your target market in mind when communicating. Speak their language. If your target audience is attorneys, and you love surfing, then they aren't likely to respond and resonate with words such as *dude* and *chillin'*. You must communicate as they do. Understand how they think and talk.

They find comfort in you when you speak their language.

Your brand doesn't need to mean something to everyone. It doesn't even need to be known by everyone. It only needs to mean something to the right ones, the people who are most likely to turn into your customer. They are the people that matter; the rest are irrelevant.

6

The Right Position

THE NUMBER ONE GOAL OF YOUR MARKETING should be to establish and position yourself as an authority in your industry or field. Authority leads to easier sales, more opportunities.

Flashy marketing campaigns and high-pressure sales tactics are no longer effective. Today your success depends on your ability to position yourself as the go-to authority in your field.

Let me stress that there is a difference between an expert and an authority. An expert is someone who knows a lot about something. An authority is someone people listen to when they speak. Being an authority is about more than your expertise. It's about your influence.

If you can't communicate your expertise, you'll never be influential. Communicate frequently and consistently. Simplify so they can take action; otherwise, it's just noise.

Positioning is about what makes you different and where you fit in the marketplace. It's all about what prospects think of you.

You don't want to be perceived as having no clear position in the minds of your prospects. You don't want to fit in with what everyone else is doing. Offer prospects a better product or service than everyone else.

> The most important element of branding is positioning.

21

Everything you do should fit in with your positioning. Positioning matters whether you are big or small. The right positioning will give you a strong brand image.

7Up is known as the "un-cola." It is their position in the market-place. It is different and is accurately positioned as being different. In the crowded beverage industry, 7Up has found their place. They've taken their position and ran with it.

A question that often comes up about being an authority in an industry is what if there is already an authority? Chances are there are already several people positioned as authorities in your field. Is there room for you? Just because there is already an authority in your field doesn't mean there isn't any room for you.

If someone got to where you want to be first, don't panic. Being first is often overrated. Coca-Cola was there before Pepsi, and Pepsi is still a major success. It's certainly not bad to be the first to do something. But it's not a requirement to be successful. It's better to be unique than to be first. Can you remember which band came out first, the Backstreet Boys or NSYNC? I sure as heck can't. All I can remember is that thankfully they went away about the same time.

> Don't strive to be first. Strive to be the best.

The difference between you and a competitor may be slim. But it's that difference that counts. That difference means the world to prospects and how they view you. The language you use, where you advertise, your customer service, website, and so on, all have an effect on your positioning. Each element of your business and brand contribute to it.

What you do is the most important factor in branding success. What you do matters way more than what you say. Make a promise you can deliver on, one that prospects will believe. To be viewed as the go-to authority in your field, you have to walk the talk.

When you are one of the leading authorities in your field, you attract business. When people have a need for you they will choose you and reach out to you because of your brand positioning.

Proof is what makes you an authority. Information is like a new form of currency. The more information you share, the more you'll be positioned and viewed as an authority. Bringing new ideas to the table and people acting on those ideas: that's proof.

You must position yourself as something different to your audience. You need to become someone your industry wants to revolve around. Be a leading authority in your field.

The world is full of generalists. Be genuine in serving people and be the go-to person in your world. Be an authority.

7

The Master Plan

I LOVE TO SELL. I love the art of selling. But I also know that I will always sell more when I give first. A strong brand is built on trust. No one will trust a brand that offers little value while cramming a pitch down their throat. Nobody likes to be pitched to over and over. I'm not saying you can't pitch; by all means, do. You'll have to if you want to survive and thrive.

But you must change your game plan. It is far more effective to give something of value away before you ask for the sale. Most businesses try to sell right out of the gate. Before you ask someone for money, you have to provide them with value first. Inform. Then sell.

No one woke up this morning and said, "I hope someone tries to sell me something today!"

Understand that the person who delivers the most value wins. You beat out your competition by providing more value than them, especially upfront. You must educate and help your audience more than your competition does. Prospects will gravitate toward those who help them out.

I was speaking at an event once that featured a solid lineup of speakers. It was a marketing event where each speaker was allowed to sell their products at the end of their presentation. While eating breakfast with the other speakers, I couldn't help but hear one them bragging about how well he sells from the stage. He was very confident, that's for sure.

As it turned out, this guy spoke right before my time slot. Each speaker was allotted 60 minutes for the presentation and sales pitch. This guy used 15 of his minutes for his content. The remaining 45 minutes were spent talking about his product and why you should buy it. I was sitting in the back of the room shaking my head.

My presentation followed his and I spent the first 55 minutes of my presentation on content. The last five minutes I showed the audience what my product was, told them what it would do for them, and passed around the order forms. I outsold the other guy 3 to 1. Deliver more value than your competition, and you will beat them every single time.

Don't be afraid to help people out upfront by sharing great information. If people are digging what you have to say, then they are also going to like what you have to sell them. They will want to take that next step.

Add your insight to what is happening in your industry. You want to regularly share information with your target audience that is relevant and beneficial to them. Help your audience understand and interpret news and information. This is incredibly valuable to them. It will continue to position you as a resource and not just a service provider. (It's far more effective than constantly promoting yourself and trying to sell upfront.)

A mortgage broker, for example, should always let the audience know how changes in interest rates affect them. Keep them up to speed on market changes and educate them. This is being a resource and not just another person trying to sell something.

Always strive to give away great information that is highly valuable. The more value you can give, the better. If your audience doesn't get value out of it, then you will be ignored and your efforts will go to waste.

The hard part is that you don't decide whether or not something is valuable. Your audience does. If they don't see or perceive any value from your message or content, they will move on and ignore you. Therefore it's imperative that you strive to provide enormous value and you do it consistently. Not every piece of content will be a home run, and that's okay.

Value isn't easy. It has to be relevant and helpful. Don't create content or a message strictly hoping someone will digest it and come running to buy from you. The most valuable content is genuine and transparent. Asking for the sale immediately after your "free, helpful content" makes you a phony. Don't do it.

Something magical happens when your audience finds you and your content to be genuinely helpful: They trust you. They value your message and thoughts. Now they will buy from you and be excited to do so.

The expectation that a customer will purchase is where most businesses get it wrong. Helping people first without any strings attached will cause people to like it, share it, and want to know more.

Sales are the by-product of giving away valuable content that is relevant to your target audience.

Again, I love selling, but there has to be a balance. I'm not sure there's a magic number, but I like to follow the 80/20 rule. So I like to have 80 percent of my marketing efforts be great content while the remaining 20 percent is left for the pitch. This works best when your content is actually good, of course. Don't put out crap. If your content sucks, it doesn't matter if you give us 10 pieces of content for each pitch. We won't buy.

Always strive to bring value to your customers and target audience. The person who delivers the most value wins. Always remember this with all you do: Value first and sell second.

8

Marketing versus Branding

LET'S GET SOME CLARITY ON THE DIFFERENCE between marketing and branding. Both are necessary to have a successful business. But there are some major differences between the two.

Some people focus all of their efforts on marketing. They don't think of themselves as a brand and therefore put zero focus on establishing their brand. They blindly ignore the effect of their brand on their business. They fail to grasp this critical fact:

> The *way* you market yourself matters.

Some people appreciate and respond to aggressive marketing. Some people despise it. How you market yourself and your products has an effect on the way people view your brand. You have to make sure that your marketing efforts are in line with what your brand is all about.

GoDaddy.com likes to run ads and commercials that are provocative in nature. These ads have nothing to do with registering domain names, but they do leave an impression on people. Whether or not that impression is good is up to each individual. But it certainly creates strong feelings about their brand, whether good or bad.

Each and every marketing effort should be congruent with your brand. If you run an ad with the headline line "Sex," and the next line says. "Now that I've got your attention, let me tell you about my brand-new thingamajig!" then you are misleading people and hurting your brand. The headline will get attention, but the damage done to your brand will be far greater than any sales you may make.

Call me crazy, but I don't like unexpected and uninvited visitors to show up at my house. One night some members of a local church showed up at my house unannounced. I'm a Christian and don't hold it against anyone trying to spread the word, but I wasn't happy to see them. I was polite about it and kindly explained to them that unexpected visitors weren't exactly my cup of tea. They understood and went on about their business.

Guess what? They came back. Not once, not twice, but three more times! It was always in the evening when my wife and I were just about to eat dinner and watch *Survivor*. The people were very nice and their church is fantastic. Their marketing efforts are not. The way they market themselves affects their brand.

My friend Scott Stratten once said, "We have to stop marketing to people the way we hate to be marketed to." Truer words have never been spoken.

Just the other night the phone rang, and it was someone with the Fraternal Order of Police asking for a donation. We love the police and have donated in the past, but the timing of this call wasn't good. It was in the evening while my wife and I were putting the kids to bed. My wife told the gentleman we weren't interested, to which he responded, "Ma'am, we're not selling blenders here. This is for the police."

Think that kind of attitude and response has an effect on their brand? You bet it does. Think it has an effect on whether or not someone donates money in the future? Yes it does. How you market yourself counts. Every marketing piece someone comes in contact with leaves an impression on your brand. Even those who aren't purchasing your product are forming an opinion about you.

Another thing to remember is that marketing tactics come and go. Branding lasts forever. Branding is ongoing. Some marketing campaigns succeed and some of them fail. But a strong developed brand lasts 24/7 all year long.

Branding is all about emotion. Most marketing campaigns are lacking both emotion and passion. There's nothing for people to get attached to. In fact, people rarely if ever feel an attachment to an individual marketing campaign, but they do feel an attachment with certain brands.

9

Do You Believe?

WARNING: THIS SECTION TEETERS DANGEROUSLY CLOSE to sounding like a motivational speaker. This isn't my intent, but pay close attention because how much you believe in yourself plays a huge factor in how successful your brand will be.

Self-belief is the best strategy I know. When you are full of self-doubt, you will have a very hard time moving forward. It will hold you back more than you can possibly imagine. Self-doubt is the number-one cause of failure for most entrepreneurs.

Self-doubt leads to fear. Fear keeps you from ever taking action. Fear keeps you from progress. Fear keeps you from success. Fear keeps you from happiness. It's impossible to be 100 percent fearless. Anyone who tells you otherwise is a numbskull. You'll never get rid of it completely, so choose something better to fear.

> If you're going to be afraid, be afraid of being poor.

Without self-confidence, you'll constantly struggle. No one wants to spend money on someone who isn't confident. Your belief in your products and services matters a lot. It shows that you have great pride in what you have to offer.

You have to be confident in what you do. You must honestly believe you are the best option for people. If you lack confidence, people will see it and they will *never* become buyers. If you're not confident in what you do, how can you expect prospects to have any confidence in you?

> No one is going to respect your opinions if you don't.

Success for your brand is greatly determined by your beliefs and not your circumstances. No excuses are acceptable. As the saying goes, you have to believe in yourself before you can expect anyone else to. Take this to heart. Customers and employees will pick up on your confidence or lack thereof. They will either become confident in your business or lose faith in it. They will feed off you.

I admit I have struggled a great deal with self-confidence in my career. People in business tell you to trust your gut instinct and to listen to that voice in your head. I heard that little voice loud and clear. It kept asking, "What if the voice in my head is an idiot?"

Although I'm not certain, I think that little voice in my head was out to get me. Everything he said had to do with self-doubt. It's bad enough that I have to deal with my obsessive-compulsive thoughts every day to then throw this little paranoid voice on me as well.

During this time when things seemed like they just weren't going my way, progress was slow. I was working hard, but I kept sabotaging myself. Sounds crazy I know. Because I didn't have confidence in myself, I never took action on my ideas. I was focused on every reason an idea wouldn't work, rather than focusing on every reason why it would.

I reached out to a good friend and mentor of mine, Danny Griffin. He has spent years studying the importance of mindset for entrepreneurs. The right mindset will propel you to success. The wrong mindset will keep you from ever getting started. Danny helped me realize I was allowing fear to control me. I remember him saying something I will never forget. My business lives by this attitude. He said, "Play the game like there is no other option but success."

It was time for a change. I began to work harder on myself than I was working on my business. Over time I developed a great sense of self-belief, and my confidence grew. The positive effect this had on my business was instant. I began playing the game with extreme confidence. I wasn't worried about whether or not I had the talent, skills, or whatever kind of mojo I thought was needed.

How confident you are in your product or service determines how aggressive you will market it. If deep down you know your product is not 100 percent awesome, you will be tentative with your marketing approach. Being timid isn't going to get your brand at the top of the food chain. When you lack confidence you lack the courage to try new innovative ideas.

No matter what industry you are in, you are in a competitive environment. It's easy to allow yourself to become intimidated by your competition. Don't worry about larger competitors. Believe in yourself and trust your abilities.

You need to have the mindset that people would be foolish not to buy your product or service. You might not want to come right out and say that, but you should be thinking it. If you are not the best at what you do or at least are working your butt off to become the best, then what's the point?

I should stress that I'm talking about confidence and not cockiness. Confidence is attractive. Cockiness is not. It is never cool to be an arrogant jerk. No one wants to work for that guy, and no one wants to do business with that guy. Believing you are the best in what you do is all about confidence in yourself, never arrogance.

Spencer Shaw relied greatly on self-belief when he dove into an industry he knew nothing about. Spence is a serial entrepreneur who runs several businesses in various niches. One day Spence began looking into the mixed martial arts industry. He saw a passionate fan base that was devoted to a sport that is growing at a rapid pace.

There was just one catch. Spence had never even seen a mixed martial arts fight before. He knew little to nothing about it. However, he didn't let that stop him. He had confidence in his research and had confidence in himself as a marketer. Simply put, he knew he would make it work.

Today, Spence works with and sponsors several professional fighters as well as launching a clothing line targeted toward mixed martial arts fans. In a short time he became a brand to be reckoned with despite his unfamiliarity with the industry. He had no reason to be confident.

He had every reason to let self-doubt and fear stop him. If he didn't believe in himself, he would have never reached his goals.

Exude confidence in all that you do. Be confident in your content, in your product, in your expertise. Your target audience will be greatly attracted to your business and will be more responsive to your marketing efforts.

It's easy to be confident in what you and your business have to offer when you are adding value. Be honest with yourself. If you are not putting out the best possible product you can or if you are not offering the best service you are capable of, reevaluate your business and make the necessary adjustments. How are you playing the game?

10

Anchor Belief

IT'S TIME TO DRAW A LINE IN THE SAND. The time for you to share your viewpoints with the world is right now. I have no doubt in my mind you have a strong stance on something in your industry. Whatever you do, don't hold that opinion back!

Don't be afraid to take a stand.

Agreement with how things have always been said and done is not only boring; it slams the door shut on innovation. It leaves you very little room for creativity. Innovation and creativity are what keeps your brand fresh.

Sometimes you've just got to rant and rave. People love people who are passionate. When you feel strongly about something and your passion shines through, then your audience will get behind what you believe in.

When you are confident in your message and take a stand on something, you are standing out and positioning yourself as an authority.

> Your brand must stand for something.

Fans are very attracted to a strong stance on something. All great brands have a point of view. A brand's philosophy or anchor belief, as I call it, is that thing that motivates you to do what you do.

Your brand's anchor belief is your brand's philosophy or viewpoint. It's a big idea that is the focus of all of your products, services, marketing, presentations, and any other element of your business. Its premise becomes the backbone of your brand.

Any brands that can identify and develop their own anchor belief will end up making a lot of money and find themselves ahead of the pack.

Your anchor belief is presented in a way that is new and interesting. It makes your target audience eager to find out more about you and your business. It helps cut through the marketing noise and becomes a valuable asset for your brand.

Your anchor belief is exciting. It's exciting for you and those who are exposed to it. It makes people want to share it because they agree with your philosophy and stance in the marketplace.

You must be completely focused on your anchor belief. It helps define your brand and gives prospects clarity about you. This is why it's absolutely critical to ensure your philosophy and message is a part of all you do, whether that be a marketing campaign, video, blog post, product, webinar, or presentation.

Because your anchor belief is unique to you, you create distance between you and the rest of the competition. It gives you great leverage in building and strengthening your audience and community. You create positioning that is unique to you.

When people attach themselves to your anchor belief, you not only create brand advocates but you establish yourself as a leader and authority. This enables you to sell more of your product or service and opens the door for more opportunities.

It's easier to get someone to buy into your philosophy and anchor belief than it is to buy a product. Once they've bought into your philosophy, it is super easy to sell your product.

Keep your message simple. Prospects hate complexity and confusion with a passion. Confused prospects will never buy from you.

11

Death of the Mundane

THINK BACK TO WHEN you first had that tiny spark that made you want to go into business or become an entrepreneur. Remember that fire of excitement that went deep down to your core? Your enthusiasm was unshakable. There are two questions I would like to ask you: What happened to the intensity of that fire? Is the fire even still lit?

Most brands are mundane and stale. Businesses, their employees, and even their customers are just going through the routine. Nothing is exciting anyone. It's time to put a stop to all of that. It's time to show the world your passion for what you do and let all the other mundane brands lay in your wake.

That fire that was there when you first started had better still be there because that fire is contagious. People feed off passion, enthusiasm, and energy. They are contagious. Your customers and your employees love to see those elements in your brand.

Most businesses are afraid to show their passion or they lose it somewhere along the way. They begin to feel cold and out of touch. There is no life in their brand.

If you are not so fired up and excited that you can't sleep at night, then don't expect anyone else to get fired up about your business either. If your brand lacks passion and emotion, your clients will lack it as well. People who are passionate about something are passionate about it on deep levels. They want to connect with people who share that passion. It excites them. You want your customers to be excited!

Mike Wolfe stars on the TV show *American Pickers*. In the show Mike and his partner go around and dig through people's barns, basements, and attics looking for pieces of history. It's a business for Mike because he sells the items later for a profit. But if you watch even 10 minutes of the show, you see his passion. His love for American history cannot be questioned. Even if it's not your cup of tea, you can't help but admire him and relate to him because of his enthusiasm. After all, the man gets super excited to dig through dirt and junk hoping for that one item he's never seen before. Because Mike's passion is easy to see, people from all over the world who share that passion call him about the items he may be interested in. Like attracts like. Passion attracts passion.

Make sure your brand isn't lacking emotion. When you begin to lose that fire inside of you, you start to settle on a mediocre business. That can lead to a mediocre life, which is unacceptable.

My friend Travis Robertson of DontSettle.org helps people relight that fire by getting them to not settle on any area of their life that isn't where they want it to be. Travis knows the importance of keeping that fire alive. Travis's passion toward helping people is both contagious and inspirational. He not only believes his mantra of "Don't settle," he lives it. His passion about the movement he has created is clear. You don't have to look hard to see it. That's the way movements start: from passion. He wants to help people get out of a cycle of just running through the motions. Your business needs to get out of that cycle as well.

A passionate fan base is a great thing for a brand. If you expect people to be excited about your message, you need to show that you are excited about it. Listen to Richard Branson in any interview and you can hear his excitement for business in his voice. After all of his success over the years, that fire inside him is still there. This not only makes consumers want to buy Virgin products, but it attracts employees who are passionate. They buy into the concept because they know how much it means to Richard. The emotions attached to the Virgin brand run through each employee in every business sector they are in.

As the leader of your brand, it all starts with you. Don't let your passion die. Too many businesses are without it already. You want to be at the core of your community. All great brands have a great leader. Steve Jobs of Apple clearly has passion. His employees do as well. They don't just believe in the products they sell. They are passionate about them. Apple fans are passionate. For years my brother made fun of me for not having a Mac computer. My brother making fun of me is nothing new, so I ignored him for a long time. Then I finally gave in and bought myself a MacBook Pro. He was so passionate about it, I figured I needed to give it a shot. I instantly became an Apple fan boy. Today every computer I own is a Mac, and you can bet there are a few iPods and iPhones in my house as well.

Is your brand worth talking about? Is your message worth sharing? The answer to these questions must be a resounding, "Heck, yeah!" If you're not dying to tell the world about what you do, then you need to reevaluate what it is you do.

The passion with Apple starts with Steve Jobs. For your business it starts with you. Don't be another mundane brand that lacks enthusiasm. Stand against that. Inspire people. Lead people. Keep that same motivation and enthusiasm you had when you first started.

12

The Creation Story

WHAT'S YOUR STORY? Your target audience is asking that question. How well you tell your story matters. Your creation story is the story of how you got to be where you are now, both in life and the creation of your business. People love to know how something came about and how it got started—from Walt Disney humbly saying, "It all started with a mouse" to the stories of Steve Jobs building computers in his garage.

These creation stories fascinate us and give us a better understanding of you and your brand. Every time someone is introduced to you for the first time they are wondering. "Who is this person?" Your creation story answers that.

Ree Drummond is known as the Pioneer Woman. She's a highly successful author and blogger. Her fan base is quite large and very passionate. Whether it's trying out recipes from her cookbook or devouring a new blog post about her children, they can't wait for what Ree will do next. So why "the Pioneer Woman"? Ree grew up in the city. She ended up marrying a real-life cowboy, and now this city girl is living on a farm learning how to create good ol' country meals. Her books and blog cover what it's like diving into her newest adventures. It's a fantastic creation story that people find interesting, and it gives them an idea of what she's all about.

We've all heard the stories of Coca-Cola being created by a pharmacist or that the Post-It Note was invented by accident. We've heard about Michael Dell selling computers from his college dorm. We've heard about rapper and businessman Jay-Z growing up in the projects and living a very hard life until his music career took off. Every successful brand has a creation story they share.

You don't have to have one of the biggest brands in the world to showcase your creation story. Tyler Ridings is the creator of the TuneVault, which creates an online backup for your iTunes library. It's impressive enough that Tyler started this business while he was still attending college. But his creation story comes from frustration followed by inspiration. Like any 15-year-old freshman in high school, Tyler had a rather large collection of music stored on his computer. Then it happened. One day his music collection crashed and he lost it all. Over six hundred hard-earned dollars down the drain in a flash. Once the anger and frustration died down, the idea for the TuneVault was born. Tyler's creation story allows us to know a little more about him and to learn that, like his audience, he's a music lover. His mission now is to save fellow music lovers from the frustration of losing their entire collection.

My good friend James Reynolds is another example of someone with an interesting creation story. He had a successful career as a photographer when he was asked to take photos of an Internet marketing event. While spending time snapping photos, James was letting all of the information being shared by the speakers sink in. Most photographers would have just showed up, done their job, and left. Not James. A spark inside of him had been lit. After the event he left his job as a photographer and started an Internet marketing consulting business. In less than 12 months he built a six-figure business helping others with their online marketing.

Everyone has an original beginning to their brand. Sure, there will be some similarities. Just think of all of the similar rags-to-riches stories out there. But no one has lived your life but you. Therefore no one has the same creation story as you. Your path in life hasn't been the same as everyone else. Your background and personality make you unique. They make your creation story unique. Don't hide it from the world. Share it and own it.

As you define your story, people will look for similarities with the struggles they have been through themselves. This tightens the bond they have with you. People relate more to your struggles and the challenges you've overcome than they do your accomplishments.

Tell the truth of how you got to this point. Let the world know how and why your business started in the first place. Make it interesting, but don't lie or exaggerate your story. You may think your story is boring, or maybe you feel it's nothing special. What matters is what your audience thinks. Let them be the judge. I used to think my own creation story was boring because it wasn't one of those "from homeless to millions" stories we hear so much about. Your story may not tug at people's heartstrings, but that doesn't mean it's not a good story.

My own creation story begins when I was a teenager. Like any 16-year-old kid, I was obsessed with reading books about branding and marketing. You can imagine how popular I was with the ladies. I'd love to tell you that while other kids dreamed of growing up to be a firefighter or astronaut, I was dreaming of being an international branding consultant. But that wasn't the case. Although I was very interested in branding and marketing, I was not focused on it for a career.

I was focused on playing in a rock band and sleeping until noon. Fast-forward a few years later, and I found myself in real estate, not having a clue what I was doing. Real estate was not my passion. One of the main reasons I became a real estate agent was because it seemed like a respectable enough career. After all, I'd be wearing a tie, so surely I'd be seen as a professional. But there was a big problem with the beginning of my real estate career: no one knew who I was. The phone wasn't ringing, even though I had some fancy business cards I gave out everywhere. It was a competitive industry full of agents who had 30 years or more of networking connections. I was 22 years old, and all of my connections were just out of high school and still living with their parents.

This is when the light bulb went off. I put to use all of that information I'd gathered from years of reading about branding and marketing and started to build my own brand. In no time I had a team of agents working for me and was generating over 400 new leads every month. It was during this time I began consulting with other real estate agents and then entrepreneurs and business owners, helping them build their own brand. I had found my passion, and the rest was history.

A great example of just how powerful your creation story can be is Dyson vacuum cleaners. When inventor James Dyson first introduced his revolutionary vacuum cleaner, the entire TV commercial was James telling his creation story. He explained what was wrong with old vacuums and how long he worked on creating a solution. It stood out not only because the Dyson vacuum is a good product, but because we got to see the person behind the idea and how it came about.

Your audience wants to know how and why you got to this point. They also want to know where you are going. As your creation story gives people insights about you, it strengthens the bond and relationship with your audience. Don't hesitate to share your creation story with people. You may think no one cares, but your audience cares a great deal about it. They will remember it, and, most importantly, they will share it.

13

Extra Ordinary

MOST BRANDS ARE BORING. Why? Because boring is easy to do. Few are willing to do something unique, and even fewer have a distinct point of view. Everyone is trying to stand out. Everyone is fighting for the same attention. Everyone is doing the same thing. It's easy to get lost in the crowd.

> The marketplace is dying for something different.

Make what you do worth talking about, and your business will grow faster than you can imagine. Your business must have a reason for existing in the marketplace. Most businesses have no reason to validate their place in the market. They are simply another "me too" competitor selling a similar product or service like everyone else in their industry at a similar price.

If the only people who would really miss your business if it went under are either related to you or your closest friends, you may have a "boring" problem. Don't misunderstand me. It's not that you can't be a dentist or sell shoes or do something that others do. It's that you can't do those things in the same way as your competitors and hope to have a brand that people feel like they need to feel complete.

Identify what makes you different. Any brand has the potential to be and do something remarkable. You must point out what you have to say that's unique and what you do that's different.

Solve problems for people. Make their lives easier. Have a reason your business exists in the marketplace. If you're just going to be like everyone else, then what's the point?

You either stand out or you are invisible. There is no in between. If you're not fascinating enough to attract an audience of avid fans, you might as well not exist. Sometimes you have to be bold and daring. If your brand isn't worth talking about, then you are going to struggle to find success no matter how much money you throw at marketing your business.

Everyone these days has attention deficit disorder (ADD). When I was in school it was called "wild," but today it's called ADD. With attention spans as short as they are, and with so many brands and messages competing for what little attention they can attract, you must be fascinating so that people stop and take notice. Being fascinating to your target audience is how you *earn* their attention.

The world is overcrowded with brands and marketing noise. It doesn't have any room for passive brands that are playing the "me too" game. If you can't rise above the noise and stand out, then any success you happen to achieve is likely to be very short lived.

Being remarkable doesn't have to be expensive or sexy. Sometimes the simplest ideas make the greatest impact and will set you apart from the crowd. Netflix is a remarkable company. They changed an entire industry with a rather simple idea. Netflix didn't change the product; their movies are the exact same ones you would get if you rented them anywhere else. They changed the way we receive the product. It's a simple change that gave them a reason to exist in the marketplace. If they had opened a physical location right next to a Blockbuster store, then what would be the point? Their value proposition would have been "Hey, we rent movies too."

Netflix avoided becoming another "me too" competitor by doing something remarkable. They did something worth talking about. They had a reason for being there.

Interestingly enough, Redbox did the same thing by basically creating a movie rental vending machine. Each time, Blockbuster was caught off guard and got stuck trying to play catch up. And each time, Blockbuster offered an inferior, "me too" product in an effort to compete. It failed. The company declared bankruptcy late in 2010.

Whatever it is that makes what you do unique must be something that benefits the prospect. It has to be something they care about. For example, I've seen a lot of businesses position themselves as environmentally conscious or "green." Is that enough to make a prospect choose them over a competitor?

That depends on whether or not it is important to the prospect. If the target audience were environmentally conscious as well, then being green would be attractive to them. If the target audience doesn't really care about environmental issues on a strong level, then being green might not matter to them, much to Al Gore's disappointment.

What makes you remarkable is that you do something for people that no one else does or you do it in a way they can't help but talk about. What makes you remarkable is doing something unique that people care about.

I think what's hard for most people to get about creating a remarkable brand is that they think it has to be some extraordinary idea or concept the world has never seen. That couldn't be further from the truth. A remarkable brand is one that does something so much better than the competition that people can't help but talk about it.

Zappos became a remarkable business without creating some new life-changing innovation. They are remarkable because their customer service is phenomenal. They've created a culture within their brand that makes them stand out from everybody else. Did Zappos invent providing great customer service? Of course not. But because people have become conditioned to expect ordinary, Zappos was able to stand out by being extra ordinary.

Every business offers some form of customer service. Zappos made theirs worth talking about. They made it easy. They made it fun. They went that extra step. What industry norm can you make extra ordinary? Zappos created a return policy that was the opposite of normal. You can return a product with absolutely no hassle, up to 365 days after you purchased it.

Too often brands end up copying other brands. This only makes brands more common and gives you the opportunity to stand out.

Never copy what another brand is doing. When you copy another brand, you become a generic version of their brand. Copycat brands have no influence.

Instead of trying to be like the biggest brands in your industry, try to be the opposite. There is always a way to differentiate your brand from the rest. It could be through packaging, colors, smell, experience, or anything. But there must be a reason and a benefit to the customer for being different. You can't just say, "My widget is red, the competitors is blue, so mine is different." It doesn't work that way.

> Being different isn't enough. There must be a reason for it.

Stop trying to be so ordinary. Normal has been done already. The last thing you want is for your brand to "fit in" with the other brands in your industry. Don't be like everyone else, no matter what. Find your style. Because most brands are so bland, you'll find standing out to be easier than you think.

Define yourself and your purpose. Broadcast your strengths. Give people a reason to pay attention to you. It's your choice to do something worth talking about or not. The only people who stand out are those who want to.

14

Bring the Noise

REGARDLESS OF WHAT KIND OF BUSINESS you are in, you must learn to think and act like a marketer. You have to know how to market effectively and promote your brand. Those who know how to run a successful brand campaign are the same ones dominating their field.

Self-promotion is promoting and marketing yourself, your products or services, skills, abilities, and accomplishments. The goal of self-promotion is to increase your visibility, grow your following, and attract more opportunities.

Please don't tear up when I tell you this because then things will be awkward, but no one is searching for you. No one is bending over backward, going out of their way to learn all about you. That is why it is up to you to get yourself out there.

I don't care how modest you are. You have to bring the noise.

You have to scream from the rooftops so that people know exactly who you are and what you do. Being a wallflower brand isn't going to get you the results you are after. You have to come at the world with all you've got, and sometimes you've got to get in their face. Now is not the time to sit back and pray people stumble across you. Don't leave your success up to chance. Bring the noise!

Four-Letter Word

Let me be perfectly clear that when I talk about self-promotion and bringing the noise, I am not talking about bragging. "Brag" is a dirty word that our society frowns on. There is a huge difference between bragging and self-promotion. Donald Trump has built a very large brand both for his company and his own personal brand. Although there are a lot of things Trump does well to build his brand, he is too boastful about it. He takes credit for things he had little to do with and constantly claims to be the best at anything he does.

Don't be the guy who brags all of the time and is a show-off. *No one* likes that guy. Maintain a sense of humility. Even though it's "self-promotion," it is not about you. It is about your target audience.

> Marketing that is purely ego driven does not generate results.

Your brand and marketing campaigns should never be just about you. Yes, it is self-promotion, but you are promoting yourself because you have value to add to people's lives.

Self-promotion needs to be geared toward and focused on what makes you remarkable, different, and ultimately better than your competitors. Self-promotion works when people see you are doing something that benefits them.

This is going to sound a bit contradictory considering we're talking about self-promotion. A big secret of successful self-promotion is to promote others more than yourself. I often talk about my coaching and consulting clients, my friends in the industry, and others who deserve special recognition. Talking about how good your customers are is *still* self-promotion because it's still about you. Let them do the talking through testimonials.

> Self-promotion is the key to personal branding success.

The key to successful self-promotion is positioning yourself as an expert in your industry. You must be a resource for people. People want to listen to experts.

Your goal is to be recognized as a leading authority in your field. You must market yourself to achieve that. Always be on the lookout for opportunities to promote yourself.

There are numerous ways to promote yourself and your brand. Blogs, e-mail marketing, public speaking, direct mail, social media, advertising, and I could go on and on. You must constantly campaign to increase visibility, establish trust, and make the sale.

One of the best tools available to help you with your brand campaign has actually been around for thousands of years. The tool I'm talking about is . . . drum roll, please . . . a calendar!

A calendar is your best friend. Use it.

Block out time in your weekly schedule for marketing and promotion. Treat this time like an important appointment that you cannot miss. Marketing and promotion generate leads and sales. There is not a more dollar-product task you can do. Yet most people spend little time on it.

Eben Pagan, a super smart business leader, taught me the power of working in blocks. I work in two-hour blocks, and I am uninterrupted during that time. Those hours are spent with a laser focus on my marketing campaigns. I get more done in those two hours than most people do all day. Imagine what two focused, uninterrupted hours a day working on self-promotion would do to your brand. Think it would have a positive effect? You'd better believe it would.

Schedule your campaigns in advance. This way you don't miss opportunities or lose consistency. Some of my marketing campaigns are scheduled a full year in advance. By scheduling things in advance you ensure a full calendar of campaigns and promotion.

If you want to be a great brand, you're going to have to learn how to be a great self-promoter. As I said earlier, people aren't looking for you. They don't know you exist. If you want people to know you and what you do, then get out there and bring the noise! Being quiet will not get people to notice you.

15

Content Explosion

HANG AROUND ENOUGH MARKETERS and you'll eventually hear the phrase "Content is king." It may be a cliché, but this one holds some weight. Your content will not only help you build awareness for your brand, but it will also position you as an authority in your field.

The more content you have out there, the easier it becomes for your prospects to find and recognize you. The more relevant and valuable your content is, the more people will trust you.

When you publish content that is informative, relevant, and valuable to your market, you will attract prospects and over time turn those prospects into clients and raving fans, which is exactly what you're trying to achieve. People pay more attention to content than they do to advertisements. They would rather read a blog than a sales letter or special promotion.

Content comes in many forms. There is content that your audience can read, like blog posts, social media updates, articles, eBooks, reports, white papers, and so on. There's content they can hear like podcasts and audio interviews, which are always popular. Then there's content they can watch like a video or webinar. Finally, there's content they can experience, such as seeing you speak at an event. There is no right or wrong form of content. Just use the mediums that you're most comfortable with. Play to your strengths and the media your target audience prefers.

You must commit to being present both online and offline and make a commitment to producing content consistently. Every week you should be creating and publishing new fresh content. Creating content once a month will not position you as an authority. It must be frequent. Anyone can say something helpful once a month, but we follow and listen to those that stay in our field of vision consistently.

The moment you stop publishing awesome content is the moment you start losing momentum and your audience starts going somewhere else.

Content of high value is the key. You can't produce crap and expect people to like it. If it's meaningless dribble, you will do more harm than good. Your content has to be useful to them, especially if you want their money later on.

> Your content should be like a bomb; it should blow people's minds.

Give away awesome content with no strings attached. Create content so good that people miss it when you haven't updated in a while.

Hit your audience with valuable content, not sales pitches. Be helpful to them and be authentic about it. Yes, your content is designed to attract new people to your brand and yes, it is designed to ultimately turn those people into sales; however, if you are not truly helping people and are only going after the sale, then your content won't be a success. There will be people your content and information helps even though they will never become a client. There isn't a thing in this world wrong with that.

Your content isn't about you. It's about the prospect. It must be centered on helping them. You're a resource to *them*. Don't create content that is all about what you have done. Create content that is all about what your prospects can do.

Every piece of information you create should be geared toward arriving at a different result than the person is currently. Take them through the process. Give them the steps they need.

Keep your content conversational and write how you talk. Your blog posts, videos, presentations, and so on should all have a consistent feel to them so your audience knows exactly what to expect every time. Don't worry about grammar or being a good writer. People only care about the value of the content. I'm certain my high school English teachers will have a heart attack when they find out I wrote a book. The content is what counts.

Make sure your content is clear and easy to understand. Don't assume your audience knows what you're talking about. Also, make sure your content is actionable. Once someone takes action on an idea you gave them, they become a fan and a buyer.

You also want to make your content fun and sexy. It's not just how good the content is, but also how effectively you get your message across.

Create content that is fun to digest. Keep it real and personal.

By publishing messages your audience finds valuable, you position yourself as an authority in your field and become easier to find by those who aren't yet familiar with you. Publishing awesome content takes time, hard work, and consistency.

> The secret key to great content is interpretation.

Interpretation is where the value is, not on information alone. Data and information are everywhere, and they are easy to access. How that information is interpreted is where your opportunity lies. News is news. What makes one news channel better than the next? The opinion and interpretation of that news does.

You are the authority people look to for interpretation of what is happening in your niche. Don't underestimate your own opinion, and always be sure to include your two cents.

Content alone is *not* enough. There's a bazillion blogs out there with great content written by people who are flat broke. Anyone can create exciting content. Creating great content does not require a marketing budget of a big brand. A little creativity goes a long way. And your content's success comes from the combination of all your other efforts.

You must make yourself visible online, and you do that with your website, blog, videos, social media, and the content you put in those places. Spread your content around as much as possible. The better your content, the more people will help you spread it around.

It's not about blasting thousands of messages into the stratosphere hoping your audience will grow. It's about creating content that is relevant and valuable to your target audience. The more relevant your content and the more valuable your audience finds it, the more your brand will grow.

With viral content, you are hoping to ignite conversation, not sales. Sales are simply a by-product of conversation and engagement. You want content that will get noticed and get people talking because by doing that, they'll be talking about you.

> Don't just create content. Inspire people and ignite a conversation.

You don't want them to digest your content and think, "That was pretty cool; now I'm gonna go check Facebook." Inspire them to get involved in the conversation. Never view content as a one-way street, especially when the Internet is involved.

I have no interest in trying to influence people with my brand. My interest lies in *inspiring* people and yours should as well.

16

Top Yourself

IT BRINGS ME GREAT PAIN that this section of the book has to be here. Caring about people, more specifically caring about your customers, shouldn't be a good business strategy. It should be a given. It's not something you should even have to think about. Because a lot of businesses don't care or claim they care but don't act like it, people are blown away when a business shows they actually care about people.

A brand that cares stands out. This is sad but true.

Although I hate telling you that caring about people is good business, I have to stress the importance of taking care of your customers and truly caring about them. When people know you care, they think of you as a resource, one they can put trust in and buy from with confidence. When people know you care, it becomes much easier for them to believe in you. Obviously, once they believe in you, they will buy from you.

Most brands have only one intention. That intention is to simply sell their product or service. Makes sense because they are in business to make money, but it can't stop there. People don't like being "sold" to and can spot a company with that as the main objective. But many companies think they are far "too big" or "too professional" to open up and reveal any sort of personality. This is another area where personal brands have a huge advantage. When people know what you are about and how much you care, they look at you differently. They feel connected to you. They talk about you. They buy from you.

> No one talks about things or people they don't care about.

No one wants your product. They want their problem solved. If your product happens to be the solution to their problem, then fantastic, but you must make it clear it's the solution. It's up to you to make people care.

It's on you to create a brand people can care about. The first step in doing that is to care about more than just the sale. Care about them. Each and every one of them.

If you don't honestly care about your audience, you should not expect them to care about you. Many times customers are unhappy but don't say a word about it. They don't say anything because they feel like the business doesn't care. Other times people won't do business with a company for the first time because they don't know how much the company cares.

We all know Zappos cares—so much so that it's almost a cliché to mention the company in this context anymore. Even if you've never purchased anything from them, you've heard the amazing stories about the level of care they have for their customers. The experience they provide to their customers is legendary and ultimately led to the company being snatched up by Amazon for nearly a billion dollars.

What's the return on investment (ROI) on "caring"? A billion dollars. So do you care? I'm sure that you do. But do you *show* it?

Our customer service standards are too low. In this day and age, simply offering good customer service puts you ahead of the pack. Most businesses have such poor customer service that even if it's just decent, it stands out and is viewed as being great. The bar has been set way too low. How sad is that? You can instantly stand out from the competition by taking care of your customers in the same way you would take care of your friends and family (at least the ones you like). Want people bragging about your brand so much they can't stop? Offer out-of-this-world service to them. On the flip side, if your customer service flat out sucks, they will talk about your brand so much they can't stop, but you will want them to.

Consumers will buy from a competitor if they provide better customer service, even if your competition is more expensive. People will spend more when they know they will be well taken care of.

Recently I was getting my truck's oil changed at Jiffy Lube. It's important to note that the only thing I know about cars is how to drive them. I'm beyond clueless when something breaks. It shouldn't come as a surprise, then, that my least favorite thing to do in life is to get the oil changed in my truck. I don't even know why I have to do it, but my truck annoyingly beeps at me every 3,000 miles until I get it done.

Now, Jiffy Lube may care on a corporate level. But I never felt the people at my local station gave a crap about me. I used to feel like they didn't care if I did business there or anywhere else. Then they did something that proved me dead wrong. One of the gentlemen working there notified me that my vehicle had a part that needed to be replaced. He said the name of this thingamajig, but I can't remember what it was. Despite my deer in headlights look as he explained it, I nodded my head as though I knew what he was talking about. Then he said, "I wouldn't drive a single mile until you have it fixed." Jiffy Lube didn't have the tiny part in stock, so he told me where to go down the road and described what the part looked like. Again, I nodded as though I understood when in reality I had no idea what he was talking about.

As I sat in the waiting room for them to finish the oil change, frustration set in. I didn't know how to find this part and didn't have time to deal with it. Then it happened. The gentleman came in and said I was good to go and not to worry about picking up the part. "Huh?" was my response. He told me that another employee there had the part we needed on his own personal vehicle. So they took it off his and fixed mine. He told me that because the employee knew what to look for, he could get the new part for his own truck on his lunch break. Phenomenal.

They showed me they cared. They provided me with an incredible experience and a level of customer service that, sadly, is all too rare. Here's the lesson in this story: Most brands think customer service only starts when a customer has a problem. They couldn't be more wrong. If they didn't do that, I would have went about my business and never thought a negative thing about them. They took care of me because they care about people. Their actions speak volumes. Now I have no reason to believe that if I ever had a problem with Jiffy Lube they would handle it right away. They left me with an extremely positive impression of their brand.

Taking care of people when there isn't a problem and when it's not expected is a sure fire way to generate positive word of mouth. Helping people who are in a jam will do amazing things for your brand.

In the weeks leading up to a conference I was putting on, my assistant was making sure all of our ducks were in a row when we discovered the venue we had secured was pulling out on us. We were two weeks out from the event and had people coming from all over the United States to attend.

Once the feeling of panic left, we went out to find another suitable location. This was a huge challenge because we needed a certain amount of space, it needed to be close to hotels and the airport, and we weren't even giving them two weeks' notice.

We found a place I had never heard of before call e|Spaces. They provide office space for entrepreneurs who can use it whenever they want for a small monthly fee. The venue was awesome, and they had clearly spared no expense in creating an amazing environment.

But we were still faced with the challenge of availability and price. I explained to them the dilemma I found myself in, and their response was awesome. They quite simply said, "Don't worry about it; we'll take care of you. Just tell us what you need."

Most businesses would have taken advantage of it being short notice and charged me an arm and a leg. They did not. In fact, they even rented me the space on a day they are normally closed, which meant their employees had to come in on their day off. The event went off without a hitch, and the attendees loved the space.

The nice folks at e|Spaces didn't know me from Adam. We had no prior relationship. They had no reason to bend over backward to help me. Their commitment to quality customer service is clear. It stands out, and next time I hold an event, there's only one place I will call.

> Don't take relationships for granted.

Once you've formed a strong relationship with someone, it becomes very difficult for your competition to get their business. It doesn't matter that the competitor might be cheaper or even more convenient. Once a relationship is formed, it's hard to break unless you screw up. People rarely abandon a brand they have a strong relationship with and trust.

This is why it's so critical to truly care about your audience. Don't just say it in a slogan. Prove it by your actions. Actions always speak louder than words.

In January 2010 while at Disney World, my family experienced firsthand what it's like when a business cares. I've been to Disney World more times than I can count. But this time was special because we brought my sister-in-law with us who had never been. My sister-in-law was 10 years old at the time (there's 17 years between her and my wife, so don't go thinking I married young), and she had recently discovered she has type 1 diabetes. Several days into the trip we were all having a blast until one morning. We were all set to leave the hotel and go to Hollywood Studios when my sister-in-law dropped her only bottle of insulin, which shattered on the tile kitchen floor. She's upset because that was the last of her medicine and it's not like her pharmacy was around the corner. My wife is upset because there are tiny pieces of glass on the floor and she doesn't want our son, who at the time was crawling, anywhere near the floor until it had been cleaned with a mop. And I'm upset because I'm now going to be late getting to the Tower of Terror (I'm the selfish one in the family).

I make a phone call down to the front desk and explain what had just happened. The gentleman assisting me was very calm and spoke to me as if he gets this phone call all the time. We gave him the information on our pharmacy back home, and he let me know they'd get a refill for us and have it to us in a few hours. Now that, in and of itself, is amazing. But Disney didn't stop there. He asked if I needed anything else, and I explained that we were about to go to one of the parks and now we hated having to sit at the hotel until the medicine came. His response? "No problem." He told me that they would bring it to the park and call me when it arrived. I was shocked. He explained there would be a fee, but I didn't care. All I was thinking was "Tower of Terror, here I come!"

Two hours later they called and met me to deliver the medicine. I was expecting a fee of epic proportions. Much to my surprise, the fee was 20 bucks. That's it. This isn't a service Disney advertises. You won't find it online, and you won't see it in any brochure. This is Disney caring. Am I likely to visit them again? You betcha. Am I likely to tell friends, family, and everyone in my social media world about them? Yep. Heck, here I am telling you now.

Many businesses say they care. Few prove it. Going above and beyond to *wow* your customers is the right thing to do. It's good for them. And it's good for your business and brand.

17

Welcome to the Social Parade

SOCIAL MEDIA HAS PROVIDED BRANDS with an opportunity to build relationships with their audiences like nothing we have seen before. Your ability to connect with new people and deepen existing relationships can have a large positive effect on your brand. Social media is about one thing and one thing only: engagement. The brands that engage the most win.

There is no questioning how powerful social media tools can be in the building of your brand. However, if your approach to social media is off base, it will severely damage your brand. Although I am a big proponent of social media and recommend it for all brands, it's important to note that it's only right for those who commit to it. It's like driving a car. I recommend everyone learn how to drive, but if you're gonna get drunk or wear a blindfold while driving, you're abusing what could have been a good thing and you should avoid it. You'll do more damage than good.

It works only for those who use it properly, and it destroys brands when not used properly. My goal here is not to frighten you but to give you a fair warning of what you're committing to when you decide to invest in making social media a component of your branding strategy. If you're not 100 percent committed to it, then don't use it.

Not being active in a medium with the word *social* doesn't make much sense, does it?

This should be a given but it's not. I have seen people go weeks without a single update and then complain about the lack of response they receive from their "audience." I don't mean to sound harsh (yes, I do), but during your little social media vacation, we simply forgot about you. The longer you're absent from social media, the harder it's going to be to reinsert yourself into our lives and get us to care again.

On rare occasion, situations will arise that will require you to be offline for an extended period of time. First, notice I said *occasionally*. Don't go searching for a reason and then claim that I gave you license to disappear every couple of weeks. Second, if you're going to be offline for a while it's no big deal, but let us know to expect it. Don't disappear and reappear for no reason. You're not Houdini, and we're not impressed. Be active and stay active.

The biggest objection to social media is "I don't have the time." Get over yourself! You are not too busy. Everyone has 15 minutes here and there throughout any given week. You can start somewhere. Morning, evening, or whatever. Find what works for you and go with it. Marc Cuban is a billionaire and involved in multiple businesses including being the owner of the Dallas Mavericks basketball team. He's obviously very busy day in and day out, yet even he tweets 74 times a month on average. You have no excuse.

So if social media is about interaction, why are so many people and brands still trying to market their businesses without engaging with people? Instead, they are merely broadcasting message after message with little to no conversation with their audience. Look, social media is a great way to share your content, and you shouldn't be afraid of using it that way. However, the key word in social media is *social*. Your audience wants to connect with you. If your conversation is completely one sided, you will turn people off and they will tune you out. Once that happens your momentum will be dead in the water because it will be nearly impossible to recover your brand's image.

Think of it this way: have you ever been at a social gathering and you get stuck talking with some jackass who won't stop talking about himself? We all have! We look for any excuse to get as far away from him as possible and then do everything we can to avoid making eye contact with him the rest of the evening.

My point is this: if all you're doing is broadcasting your message and never engaging in conversation with your audience, you're being *that guy*. You're turning people off.

Understanding that social media success is defined in terms of engagement can empower you to succeed with it from day one. How? Simply by leveraging it to create relationships with prospects, forge bonds with industry peers, and strengthen your relationships with existing clients through online engagement. Remember, it's not about you; it's about finding ways to provide value to those you interact with. When you do that, you'll worry less about "having nothing to say" and more about how you can help those you come in contact with.

It's not always easy to begin a conversation with someone you don't know, but the Internet empowers us all to be extroverts. Don't make the mistake of always talking to the same people over and over on social media. Meet and interact with new people on an ongoing basis.

Social media also isn't the place to choose favorites. When was the last time you struck up a conversation with someone online that you didn't really know? Most people get comfortable and end up communicating with the same people time and time again. And usually these are people you are communicating with offline as well. Don't abandon your social media strategy just to chitchat with your buddies.

Your prospects would *love* to talk to you and get to know you. They also want you to get to know them. Use social media to meet new people. Some of the coolest people I know I met via social media. In fact, three of my closest offline friends met me through social media. Many of my best clients have come from social media. No more excuses—it's time to start engaging.

There is a conversation going on right now within your industry. Potential customers are talking, but are you listening? You had better be because I can guarantee your competition is. If you sell products to pet owners and you aren't paying attention to and jumping in on the conversation pet owners are having online, then you are digging your own grave. If a competitor listens more than you and engages more than you, then who do you think people will choose when it comes time to buy? You have to bring your best game. Social media is giving you the opportunity to position yourself as the go-to authority in your field. Don't blow it.

When it comes to social media, you have to be interesting. The biggest mistake you can make is to be boring. If your message isn't compelling or interesting, your efforts won't be effective and you'll waste a huge opportunity. No one likes to hang out with boring people. The same is true online. If you want to stand out and get people to pay attention, then give us something. Let us get to know you—we may end up liking you.

Not a day goes by that I don't see people ruining their brand through social media. There are a few no-no's you want to avoid. The biggest pet peeve of mine is seeing people using social media to complain. You have to realize that when you use social media to complain about your problems, you often end up looking just as bad. We have enough problems of our own without you adding yours on top of them.

On my very first day in sales, a gentleman who had been in sales for a trillion years was training me. He said something to me that I will never forget: "People don't care if your dog just died." At first, I was kind of confused and started to miss my puppy back at home. He went on to explain that people only care about how *their* day is going. They are far less interested in hearing about *your* day. He finished by saying, "People don't care if your dog died; they care if their dog died."

Social media is not your outlet to bitch and moan. No one likes hanging out with negative people. If you have a problem with a business or product, do you give them the chance to fix it before broadcasting your unhappiness with the social media world? After seeing someone complain about their popcorn at a movie theater, I asked them what the theater did to fix it. Their response was "I didn't tell them." I'm going to go out on a limb and guess that your audience doesn't care if your popcorn is good. Before you complain about someone online, give the person a chance to fix it. If they don't do anything about it, then let your anger fly!

While you're trying to make someone or some business look bad, you're damaging your brand. Several people I've been connected with have killed all chances of me hiring them or recommending them to a friend. The reason is that people like to deal with positive people.

When you complain all the time, you sound like someone who can't be pleased. Keep your bashing to a minimum, and remember that the next time you decide to slam someone or some business, you look just as bad. Keep it classy and take the high road.

Another area to be cautious about is politics. This one drives me freaking crazy. I'm blown away by how many people use social media as their soapbox when it comes to politics. If you're not trying to build a brand or a business, then by all means make a fool of yourself. But if you're trying to grow your brand and business, think twice before getting all political on your audience. When you slam the president as if all of your audience agrees, you're showing how dumb you really are. Go ahead and slam the political party you're against, and then I can congratulate you on alienating half of your audience.

You know those people who have no filter between what they think and what they say? I'm related to most of them. You must have a filter with social media.

Just because you have a voice doesn't mean you have something to say. Although you want to incorporate your personality, you don't want to alienate your target audience.

Some brands fear social media because they don't want to see negative comments. A better strategy would be to stop sucking. You are going to hear about the shortcomings of your product or service. Rather than running from this, take the feedback to heart. You now know what to fix and what to improve on. You can create a better brand by listening and then letting the world know how you've changed.

Earlier I mentioned the importance of listening. Critics of social media often question the return on investment (ROI). So what is the ROI of listening? Allow me to explain my Dream 50 Strategy, also known as my Creepy Stalker Strategy. Like many people I first thought social media was the dumbest thing to ever come out of the Internet. I'm happy I was wrong. When I first dove in, I made a list of 50 people I wanted to be connected with. These were 50 people who were in a position to help my business. They already had a following, and if I could get them to promote my brand it would be a huge boost for me. I did not previously know any of them.

I spent several months listening. I paid attention to what they wrote about. Did they have family? What sports team did they like?

I made notes of anything and everything about them. After several months of listening first, I then began to engage with them.

I spent months chatting with them online about their business and the things that interested them. If their favorite football team was playing mine, I'd be sure we had conversations about that. I let them get to know me. I wasn't asking them for help or to promote my business. We were building a relationship.

After several months of establishing a relationship and communicating regularly, most of these relationships were taken off social media and moved to communicating via e-mail or phone. It was at that point that our friendships were solid enough for us to support each other in business. After eight months of being very focused, I had secured 43 of the 50 as affiliates who would promote my business.

Three years later, and eight of my top 10 affiliates came from that Dream 50. I haven't calculated how much money they've brought in as affiliates, but it's a lot. And better yet, so many of them are close friends: friends I've partnered with in different business projects and friends that I wouldn't trade a thing for. You can't put ROI on friendships.

Because social media requires significant time involvement, people try to take shortcuts. One of the shortcuts they take is by scheduling updates to be posted automatically when they are not around. This seems harmless because, after all, you want to maintain your visibility. But it can be damaging. In fact, it hurts your brand for two reasons.

The first reason is that when someone replies to your automated post, you aren't there to interact. Over time they will stop trying to engage with you. There's plenty of other brands willing to give them attention.

Second, the timing of your scheduled updates can work against you. I've seen someone tweet "goodnight" to their followers and not ten minutes later a prescheduled tweet goes out promoting their iPhone app. It just looks silly. You also have no idea what may be happening in the world that will make your automated posts look childish.

When the announcement came that America had killed known terrorist Osama Bin Laden, the Twitter world exploded. It's all anyone was tweeting about regardless of what part of the world they were in. Yet there were people's automated tweets coming in promoting their e-book or something ridiculous. It was so obviously automated and turned people off.

Another shortcut they take is that they link their Facebook and Twitter updates together. Sometimes they even throw in LinkedIn just for kicks. This is a monumental mistake. The platforms are different. They move at different speeds and people are in different mindsets when using them.

By having your Twitter feed update every time you post on Facebook, you're essentially telling your Twitter followers you don't care enough about them to be present. You're letting them know your only concern is blasting your content at them.

Nothing good can come out of linking platforms. Trust me. I tried it and it wasn't pretty. I had my Facebook account linked with my Twitter account. Twitter was the platform I was most active on. At that time I wasn't paying as much attention to Facebook. So I began rattling off some of the following tweets:

> "Mother-in-law has been gone for 7 days & we've had 7 days of sunshine. She comes home & we have tornado warnings. Coincidence? I think not."
>
> "My mother-in-law gave us a plant called 'mother-in-law's tongue.' I'm gonna put it in 'son-in-law's trash.'"
>
> "Driving my mother-in-law's car to get lunch. I'm adjusting all of her mirrors & reprogramming her radio stations."

I posted these on Twitter, completely forgetting that they were showing up on Facebook and that my mother-in-law and I are friends on Facebook. Please don't link the two. Trust me.

Thanks to social media, large corporate brands no longer have a monopoly on marketing and reach. Personal brands can (and do) amass large followings and earn the attention of their target audience. It takes consistency and engagement to make it work. With social media people are watching every step you take. Always position yourself in the best light. Have fun and be real.

18

The Brand Conversation

TOO MANY BUSINESSES HAVE BEEN SHOVING their marketing message down our throats. It's far more annoying than it is effective. The good news is that there are people who are fighting this "machine" by engaging with their audience and building lasting relationships. And guess what? They are winning.

Everywhere you turn someone is preaching about engagement. I'm not talking about "will you marry me" engagement. There are easier ways to make a sale than marrying someone. I'm talking about engaging with your audience. It's not a new concept by any means; however, so many brands fail to engage with people that I have to bring it up.

Regardless of the demographics of your market, they want to hear from you. Interacting with people brings big rewards. It strengthens your relationship with them and the level of trust they have with you. It also brings others in because they want to be a part of the conversation. Nobody likes to be left out.

Engagement shows you care. You don't have to be their best friend and chat with every single person in your audience every day. You wouldn't have any time left.

As social media has changed the marketing landscape, people have now come to expect engagement. Be aware that even those who are not actively engaging with you are watching to see how fast you respond and engage with others.

Relationships are a major component of successful brands. You never know when a relationship will come in handy, so be cautious about burning bridges. Don't write someone off. They may become very successful at a later date. Even the most unlikely of people could end up in a position to help you one day.

I was attending a marketing conference that featured Gene Simmons from the rock band KISS as the keynote speaker. I'm not exactly a KISS fan because they were before my time, but I'm obviously aware of them and know who Gene Simmons is. He is far more than a rock-and-roll star, although he is certainly that. Gene is a savvy entrepreneur and marketer whose licensing deals with KISS have brought in millions.

I honestly did not know what to expect from Gene. Was he going to come on stage in 10-inch metal boots while fire shoots out behind him? I was half expecting full KISS makeup and him waving his tongue at us. Gene hit the stage and was completely normal. No makeup. No fire. No tongue.

But what was truly amazing about Gene beyond his entrepreneurial skills is that he was alone. No bodyguards, no posse, no entourage. Everyone was shocked to see a celebrity so easy to access. Gene was asked why he traveled that way, and he responded by saying something I want you to never forget.

He said, "Because there's not a single person on this planet that I can't learn something from."

Everyone matters. Gene went on to share a story about how he once came up with a brilliant marketing idea after having a brief conversation with a taxicab driver. It doesn't matter how big your brand gets. If you stop engaging with people, you will miss out on a lot.

The larger a brand gets the more it seems to lose touch with its core audience and customers. The brands that are remarkable and stand out are the ones who never lose that touch. Never stop connecting with people. Ever.

> Interactions, not interruptions, are the key to marketing.

If you want your brand to be a huge success, developing a strong relationship with your target audience is a must. Have patience. Let the relationship mature.

Frequent communication with your target audience lets them know that you value the relationship. It allows you to get to know them. How can you serve and provide value to your customers if you don't even know them?

The better you know your customers, the better you can create valuable content and products for them. There is no point in guessing, and making assumptions about your audience is extremely dangerous.

The brand that communicates best wins. Brands that engage with people are more successful than those that do not. If someone reaches out to you, respond! It's an honor when someone leaves a comment on your blog or sends you an e-mail or converses with you through social media. If you don't respond and actively engage with them, they will quickly stop reaching out to you and go find someone who will communicate with them.

19

Many Shades of You

"IT'S NOT PERSONAL, IT'S BUSINESS." What a huge joke this quote is. I'm not sure who originally said it, but he or she is wrong. Unless you're reading this in the year 2452, you are a person. Everything is personal because it's people we are doing business with.

We like it when businesses and people show their personality. It adds a human element that far too many businesses are lacking. A little personality goes a long way, so feel free to let your hair down.

People do business with people. People they know, like, and trust. They especially buy stuff from those they like. People enjoy spending time with people they like and people who are like them. There is nothing new about that. But brands with no personality fail to realize that people buy from people they like.

Putting your personality into your marketing and business isn't just about getting people to warm up to you. It's a strategy that you have to act on if you want to survive.

> The *only* difference between you and your competition is your brand.

Anyone can copy your website or knock off your product or service. They can steal your brand colors and can rip off your content. There is only one element of your brand competitors can never copy. They cannot copy you.

> Anyone can copy what you do, but few can copy how you do it.

You are your biggest advantage in business. What you sell may not be one of a kind, but you are. You create the value for people, not your business name or fancy logo.

Personality and charisma are a critical element to your brand. People want to get to know you. You'll attract people and customers to you when they feel like they know you. Charisma and personality are not something you are just born with. Those who have it choose to have it. It's your choice.

My father came from meager beginnings. He grew up on a farm in a small town in Tennessee that I can assure you that you've never heard of. The town he grew up in makes Mayberry look like New York City. He lost his father at a very young age, and every second not in school he spent working the farm.

After graduating high school my father moved to the "city," which was another small town outside of Nashville. Life was certainly different and faster than he was used to. To give you an idea of just how different life was for him, he and my mother went out for pizza on their first date. My dad had never heard of pizza before!

My father began working as an electrician. He was a dedicated employee who would walk or ride a bike to work every day. His work ethic that was instilled in him from a young age is second to none. Now, even though my dad is just a country boy from the middle of nowhere, he is no dummy. He knew that he wanted more in life and was prepared to go get it.

He started his own electric company with one of his brothers and immediately began working on it night and day. Like any new business, Morgan Electric needed work. It wasn't like he knew any of the homebuilders in the area who could kindly throw him a bone. Nope. If was going to get business, he was going to have to go earn it.

He had no fancy college degree to woo people with. No trail of experience to prove his performance. All he had was his personality.

You know those people who never meet a stranger? That's my dad. But more than that, he can turn a stranger into a friend in about 10 seconds.

He went job site to job site meeting builders. Making them laugh, letting them get to know him. All he needed was a shot at their business. He got several. Today, Morgan Electric is one of the largest electric companies in middle Tennessee if not the largest. It was built on the back of his personality. It was all he had. It was all he needed.

Let people see who you are. Talk how you really talk. Stop taking yourself so seriously. Let your personality and your company's personality come through in what you do.

Personal information attracts people who have similar interests as you. What seems little to you may be important to your audience. You never know which area of your personality they will relate to.

I've built great relationships within my audience when talking to them about my kids. They respond with stories about their children, and a bond is formed through the commonality. Something as seemingly irrelevant as an opinion about a sports team can open the door to new relationships. I established a relationship with a peer in my industry when we began talking trash with each other over who was the better football team, the New York Jets or the Tennessee Titans. We all know the answer to that, by the way.

> Commonalities ignite conversations.

It's okay to show your flaws and reveal your shortcomings because it lets people know you are just like them. We all have them. Sure, some of you are more flawed than the rest of us, but we all have a few. No one expects you to be perfect.

Be open about your quirks. These strange little things you do that us normal people don't, are what makes you interesting. My own obsessive-compulsive disorder, also known as OCD, provides a lot of interesting conversations with my audience. They get a kick out my quirks, such as always wearing black when I speak in public and my addiction to watches even though I rarely wear one. I'm not Howard Hughes bad, but I am related to him, so maybe my future involves wearing tissue boxes as shoes and washing my hands until they bleed.

Put more *you* into your brand, even if you're not funny or have the best personality ever. If you're not someone with an outgoing personality, don't worry. There are billions of shy quiet-type people who will relate to your personality. They are just like you.

You don't have to share everything. Heck, we don't want to know everything! Keep some things to yourself. People like a little mystery. Put out what you are comfortable sharing. Find your groove and run with it.

You draw the line on what you are willing to share and what you want to keep private. If there is an area of your life you feel uncomfortable sharing, then do not share it. It's that simple. My audience would likely be surprised to know that I'm a very private person. I share stories about my kids, hobbies, and occasionally my crazy mother-in-law, whom I'm hoping doesn't read this far into the book.

It appears as though I'm open. But the reality is that I'm a very private person. And truthfully, I just don't have that exciting of a life to share awesome stuff. My idea of fun on a Friday night is staying home and watching a movie. Not exactly the coolest story to share with my audience.

Find the balance that works best for you. Be smart about things and stay safe.

Too often people try to hide behind their brand, not realizing they are the brand. It's not uncommon to see people using a logo as their profile photos online. People want to see you. Unless you're Starbucks, don't use a logo as your profile picture.

If you happen to be hideously ugly, then I suggest making it a part of your brand. Like the "Ugly Accountant" or something. While we're on the subject of photos and proving you're a real person, let me say that a current photo of you is a must. It doesn't have to have been taken this week, but a glamour shot photo of you from 1994 is *never* a good idea.

Also use a creative bio that clearly gives a benefit to your audience and accurately describes what you do. If people ask what you do or read your bio and they get "website designer," it doesn't tell them much and doesn't stand out at all. A better bio would be "I give entrepreneurs a tool that generates more leads than they can handle." There's a benefit there.

Another bad example of a bio is something I've done myself. It's the list of everything- about- your- life bio. You know what I'm talking about. It looks something like this: Christian, Husband, Father, Entrepreneur, Golfer, Sports Fan, and Taco Lover. Yes, I'm all of those things, but do you care?

It doesn't really tell you anything, and it certainly doesn't grab your attention. My bio is "I make entrepreneurs and their businesses fascinating." It is different but also opens the door to communication.

Sharing personal stories allows your audience to warm up to you. It lets them know what you're like and what you're all about. The more friendly and likable you are, the more successful you will be. No one wants to do business with someone they don't like.

20

Celebrity Currency

WE LIVE IN A WORLD OBSESSED WITH CELEBRITIES. I'm not saying it's right or wrong. It's just the way it is. The staff of *Forbes* magazine even publish a list of the most influential celebrities the same way they do their list of influential and wealthy business leaders. It doesn't matter who your target market is, they are fascinated with celebrity. This fascination with celebrities presents a unique opportunity for you to create a level of celebrity with your brand.

> Turn your personal brand into a celebrity, and you'll dominate the competition.

You don't have to be big like Oprah. I mean big as in celebrity big, not like she's healthy big. Oh, never mind. You want to be a celebrity within your industry. Someone your audience views as a celebrity although the rest of the world does not.

In my world of marketing and branding, running into Seth Godin at the airport would be pretty darn cool. He's a celebrity of sorts to us. If my parents ran into him, they wouldn't give him a second look. The general public isn't aware Seth exists. This sounds odd because in our world he's an A-list celebrity.

Many of my clients are celebrities within their profession. They are stopped for photos and autographs repeatedly at industry events and conferences. Yet again, the vast majority of people do not know who they are, nor do they care.

The smaller your niche, the easier it is to become a celebrity to that audience. When you put yourself in all of your marketing efforts, people quickly get to know you. It's easier to raise your status because you're dealing with a smaller number of people to brand yourself to. Becoming a celebrity to a larger niche is very much attainable, but it will take a little more time as well as some big moves to elevate your status.

One of the quickest ways to elevate your celebrity status is through the power of association. Being friends with preexisting celebrities within your niche can certainly boost your celeb factor. When people see you having conversations with them and interacting with them, the power of that association links you to their celebrity. Even a photo of you and a celebrity within your industry will elevate your status. I often share photos of me with superstar celebs in my world such as Seth Godin, Dan Kennedy, Bob Burg, and George Ross (one of Donald Trump's right-hand men).

When your audience views you as a celebrity, you become more interesting to them. You become fascinating. Your presence increases as well as your media attention and opportunities.

> The majority of people are nobodies. Go be somebody.

Throughout this book I'm explaining how to position yourself as an authority. An authority with a celebrity status is very appealing to your audience. An authority is someone who knows a lot more about a certain subject than everyone else. Since I was a teenager I've read books and studied branding. I've worked with brands all across the globe. I'm an authority on this topic. I don't need a fancy designation or someone's permission to be an authority. I'm an authority because my audience says so. You are an authority on something. You don't have to be a master of a million topics or skills. You just need to focus on your one area of expertise.

When economic times are tough, people become more selective in who and what they spend their money on. As they give the purchase process more thought, they gravitate toward authority figures. They want to do business with the best. The higher your level of celebrity, the more they will beat down your door to work with you.

Because of your authority positioning and your celebrity status, you experience less objections and price resistance. This allows you to charge premium prices and ensure you get what you are worth. Imagine for a second that you want to learn how to snowboard. You do a little research and find there are a few videos that will teach you the basics. One of them is by some dude you've never heard of, and the other one, although more expensive, is by Olympic snowboarding champion Shaun White. Which one are you going to buy?

You're buying the one with Shaun White, of course. He's a celebrity in that world and has the credibility to back up his authority positioning. Price isn't an issue here. People want to do business with the best.

We are all fascinated by celebrities. Even if you think you're not, trust me, you are. I once took a few golf lessons from a very nice guy who knew his stuff. He had me hitting the ball like a pro in just a few swings. It was amazing. Yet anytime the subject of golf lessons comes up, I start thinking about how this instructor told me he once was partnered with golf legend Greg Norman in a PGA tournament. If you're a golfer, I don't need to identify Greg Norman. In fact, you may know exactly who he is even if you're not a golfer. I found it fascinating that my instructor had played a few rounds of competitive golf with Greg. Why? Because to me Greg is a big celebrity. And we love celebrities.

If the thousands of celebrity gossip magazines and websites are not enough to prove just how obsessed we are with celebrities, take a look at how often we talk about them. If you see some random guy in the mall who looks like a celebrity, you stop and tell your friends to look. If you encounter a celebrity in any way, you start dropping the name into every conversation. You want to be a name that people in your world drop in general conversation. This is the one time it's acceptable to be happy about name-dropping. Normally, I am very turned off by name-dropping. I'm sitting next to Jay-Z, and he agrees.

Your brand really takes off when there is an element of aspiration with it. People will want to be you or be friends with you. They are fascinated and excited by celebrities. Go out and be a celebrity to your audience. Have some fun with it, and use it to your advantage. It's a phenomenal way to beat out your competition in sales and opportunities.

21

The Uncommon Brand

IF YOU'VE READ AT LEAST TWO BOOKS on marketing or even branding, you have read about USPs before. A USP, or unique selling proposition, is by no means anything new. Sometimes it is referred to as a unique value proposition. I was going to rename it unique brand positioning, but do we really need another name for it? I don't think so.

What is truly amazing is that although USPs are nothing new, it is all too common to see a brand without one. Even those that do have one rarely market it properly. You don't want to be a common brand. You want to stand out and be positioned as a better option than your competition. I stress the importance of establishing your USP because I have seen it transform my clients' businesses, and I have even experienced the transformation in one of my own businesses as well.

Your USP should let prospects know why they should purchase your product or service over any competitor of yours and over doing nothing at all. It's that defining statement of what makes your brand both different and better than the rest of the competition.

Creating a USP seems like a daunting task. Understand that although your USP gives you great positioning in the marketplace, you are not married to it forever. You can always improve on it and should continually strive to do so.

Your USP is focused on something you do that no one else offers. It also must be a strong benefit to the customer. "In business since 1923" has little benefit to the customer. It doesn't say you're the best. It doesn't communicate to potential customers what you do that your competitors do not. It just says that you're old. It's not a USP. It's more of a slogan or tagline. USPs clearly showcase value to the customer.

When creating your USP, ask yourself how your product or service adds extreme value to your target audience. Make sure your USP covers the three B's:

Brief: Your USP shouldn't take you 30 seconds to spit out. It should be clear and concise. If your USP is three sentences long, you are doing it wrong.

Benefit: A USP isn't your tagline. It articulates a benefit to doing business with you. There is nothing unique about a USP that isn't benefit driven.

Believable: Although your USP should make someone stop and pay attention, it must be something they believe. "Lose 20 pounds in less than 5 minutes" is unique, shocking, and has a clear benefit. But it's in no way believable and therefore is a bad idea.

Colgate made sure to differentiate their toothpaste from the competition with their USP: "Cleans your breath while it cleans your teeth." The benefit is easy to grasp, it's different than other options, and it positions them as the ultimate package.

Domino's Pizza catapulted their business to an entirely new level when they announced their performance-based USP: fresh, hot pizza delivered to your door in 30 minutes or it's free.

The benefit is clear. None of their competitors were doing it at the time. Take note that any of their competitors could have done this themselves. They were afraid to. Often a great USP says what you do that others are afraid to.

When I was in real estate, I was up against several competitors who had more experience, bigger teams, and a more visible presence than I did. I needed my brand to stand out. I needed to showcase something I did that the competition did not. It had to be something that would cause a prospect who was thinking about selling their home to pick up the phone and call me rather than someone else.

My USP was "Your home sold in 45 days or I'll sell it for free!" It showed I was willing to put my money where my mouth was. I was willing to be held accountable to my performance. It worked like crazy. Not only did my business more than triple, but also my competitors were asking me how I did it. Of course, I never explained it to them!

They could have done it themselves, but they were afraid to. It was too bold and too risky in their eyes. I even had one real estate agent who had been in the business for more than 25 years ask me to stop advertising it. When I asked him why, he simply responded, "Because that's not the way we do it." Clearly I had hit a nerve with the competition. I also hit a nerve with my audience, who was very impressed to see someone give them a reason for their choice of Realtor.

Your USP is a claim that nobody else can make. Either they can't fulfill the promise or they are too afraid to try.

Tempur-Pedic sells mattresses. Not the most exciting business in the world, but they do an amazing job of removing the prospect's risk. They have a nice USP with their "90-Day Tryout" program. You buy the mattress, they deliver it and set it up, and then you have 90 days to decide if you like it. If you don't like it, then they reimburse you and pick up the mattress. It's a nice reason to give them a shot, but the best part is how they back it up. Studies have shown that 94 percent of Tempur-Pedic owners like their mattress. Nine out of 10 say they would purchase a Tempur-Pedic mattress again.

It's nice proof that supports their claim. Any prospect can see that Tempur-Pedic is willing to let you try it for 90 days with the risk on them because of how many satisfied customers they have. In fact, studies have also shown that on average Tempur-Pedic owners tell 14 people about their mattress. That's incredible! And Tempur-Pedic leverages it to their advantage. They recently launched a series of new advertising campaigns that challenged prospects to talk to any Tempur-Pedic owner about how he or she feels about their mattress. They are showcasing a strong USP and letting their satisfied customers back up their claims.

A good USP can put your brand on the map in a hurry. Provide proof and testimonials to back up your USP, so that prospects know they can believe it. Make sure your USP is simple and easy to understand. Don't overcomplicate it. And most of all, make sure it articulates a great benefit for the customer.

22

Dissident

SOMETIMES YOU'VE JUST GOTTA PICK A FIGHT. It can be a great positioning tool and branding strategy to be dissident and go against the majority. As is the case far too often, the popular majority is wrong. Every now and then someone needs to come along and knock them down a notch.

That person needs to be you.

If you have something to say, then say it. Especially when you know the target audience or community is thinking what you have the guts to stand up and say. People are greatly attracted to someone who is dissident. They love antiheroes.

> People respond to those who challenge the status quo.

In the late 1980s, rock music was . . . well, it was sad. It was all about hair metal bands with makeup. Bands that were constantly trying to perfect the next rock ballad. They loved being celebrities. For them it was about the attention not the music. They had no idea an antihero was about to change the industry forever.

In the early 1990s, a small band from Seattle changed music. That band, of course, was Nirvana, led by Kurt Cobain. Kurt was about the music and not the celebrity. Nirvana's sound was raw and their lyrics were real. Their look was sloppy and called "grunge" for good reason. They were the complete opposite of the hair metal bands.

Kurt quickly became labeled as the voice of his generation because he challenged the status quo. He fought the majority and found massive support from those who felt the same way as he did.

> Being outspoken and controversial works.

Scott Stratten is an antihero for the marketing world. He's the author of the book *Unmarketing*, and his brand is all about calling businesses out on the pushy ways they market themselves. Scott and I have become close friends because we both like to call it like we see it.

In my opinion, Scott is exactly what the Brand Against the Machine movement is about. By helping business owners understand that they are marketing to people and they should treat them as such, Scott has become a voice for the consumer. He's the William Wallace of marketing.

He goes against the grain of what most marketing coaches spit out. He's not afraid to speak out against those who, although popular, are doing it wrong. Scott has amassed an incredible following online and offline because people love hearing his insights on how businesses are often going about things the wrong way.

Being dissident isn't easy. Lots of criticism and hate will come your way. When you start attacking industry norms, some are going to fight back. Scott knows it's not them he's trying to win over. His only concern is his target audience. And he's winning them over in droves.

Antiheroes aren't villains. They aren't negative or angry. They just oppose the way things are normally taught or done. They have an opinion that goes against the majority.

Richard Branson's brand Virgin is all about being the voice of the people. They look for industries where service and value are suffering and come in and provide an overwhelming amount of both.

Virgin Airlines, for example, provides a lot of services that most airlines will charge you for. They maintain a small feel to their brand and position themselves as the underdog of sorts. They aren't afraid to talk about what the competition is doing wrong and how Virgin is doing it right.

Being dissident has worked for me as well. Personally, I feel that most people who talk about branding are just spouting out theory and fluff. Nothing they say has been proven. They stand for nothing. I don't want to fit in and do things the way they have always been done. I don't want you to do that either.

Branding is all about standing out. If your opinions and actions are the exact same as everyone else, you will have a very hard time standing out. You will blend in and go unnoticed.

Never be afraid to stand up for what you believe in and what you think is right. Chances are you are not the only one who feels that way. Those who agree with you will find you refreshing, and they will be supportive. Not everyone likes going with the majority.

23

Your Brand's Home Base

HANDS DOWN, one of my favorite branding tools is a blog. It's your home online and is a phenomenal tool for establishing authority positioning in your niche. I believe a blog is essential for personal brands. Corporate brands may not find a blog is the best tool, but you still need a home online.

> Your blog is your best tool to communicate the essence of your brand.

A blog is the best platform to use for your content. You can write posts, videos, audios, and basically any type of content. A blog sets up your authority and helps people know exactly what you do and how it helps them.

In general, people are more trusting of a blog than a traditional website. Your blog allows you to not only display your content and knowledge but also your personality. The typical blog post is simply good content. No sales pitch or special offers. This is why blogs are nonthreatening to people. They can get the information they need without hassle.

When you try to make a sale, people become defensive and their guard goes up. You can use your blog to sell without really selling. Let me explain.

Prospects are far less likely to buy from you when they have no trust in you. If you lack authority and credibility in their eyes, you have little influence over their buying decisions. Using your blog to showcase your content to establish that credibility and authority is critical. Your blog is a bridge to sales.

If you send out an e-mail to your audience letting them know you've just posted an awesome new post or video on your blog, you're going to get a lot of people to check it out. Because a blog is less threatening to them, they are more willing to see what you've got going on than if you sent them directly to a sales page with an order form for your product. Then at the end of the post or video, you can showcase an offer they might be interested in.

Important note: Don't make every single blog post a pitch for something. That's not the way it works. Your content must really kick ass. As people read your blog, they get familiar with you and your knowledge. If they like your content, they'll like your product or service. Use your blog to set up that authority positioning.

There are a lot different types and formats of blog posts. There is no right or wrong, but some work a little better than others. I'll quickly go over some of the types that I've found produce the best results.

I love me some video. All of the benefits of using video are in another chapter in this book. Use video on your blog as much as possible. Videos have a high-perceived value, and people get to know you better. Also, people love sharing videos, which means your blog post will get shared more.

There's a reason David Letterman's Top 10 List is so popular besides being funny. People love lists. Some of my most popular and shared blog posts were lists. They were titled "10 Reasons We Won't Do Business With You" and "7 Ways to Murder Your Brand with Social Media." People know a list is typically short and will be easy for them to digest. You can do a long list, but I don't recommend it. Every time I see a blog post titled something like "100 Ways to Increase Sales," I can't help but think that if any one of them worked, we wouldn't need the other 99.

Another popular type of blog post is to use audio. You can interview someone with expertise in your industry, for example, and share that audio on your blog. The perceived value is higher than a typical article, and it stands a chance of being shared more.

The key to a great blog post is not great content. Your content has to be killer, but it's the headline that starts things rolling. Without a compelling headline, your blog post will go nowhere regardless of how awesome it is. I spend more time working on the headline than I do the content. I know if the headline is great then people will pay attention and will be far more likely to share it.

Copywriting is a skill I highly suggest you learn. It's one of the first things I teach my clients when they start blogging. There are many wonderful books out there on copywriting that cover everything you'd want to know, but let me give you some examples of some good and bad headlines so you know what I'm talking about.

Good: 7 Secret Social Media Strategies You Can Use Today
Bad: Social Media Tips for Every Business
Good: How to Avoid This $10,000 Mistake
Bad: Don't Do This
Good: 3 Quick & Easy Ways to Rock Your Next Presentation
Bad: Presentation Tips for Your Next Presentation

A great headline stands out, invokes curiosity, and lets the reader know exactly what to expect. A blog post with a great headline and great content is a deadly combination.

Let me share one more quick blog tip with you just because I think you're awesome. Writing a blog post as a guest for someone else's blog is a fantastic way to get your brand in front of a new audience. Bloggers are always looking for content for their blog. You can make their life easier by giving them a post they can use. Start by asking around and see if any of your friends or following will let you do a guest post. Do a good job for them and you'll no doubt get new readers to your own blog.

As you can see, your blog is a great brand-building tool. Like anything, you want to stay consistent with it. Publish on a schedule that works for you. Some people blog every single day. I don't recommend it, especially if you have a life. If you post every single day, there is no way they will all be a hit. Daily blogging makes it too easy for your readers to start skipping posts. By posting frequently but not daily, you can be sure they are looking forward to the next post.

Pardon me while I go on a bit of a rant here. There are a few things that bug me that I'd like to set straight. We've gone over why you want to position yourself as an authority and all of the benefits that come from it. It's not easy to do, so be sure your efforts aren't going to waste by doing something that is killing your authority.

Let me give you an example to explain what I mean. One night while doing a live online broadcast for my audience, I thought it would be cool to do some website critiques for viewers who volunteered. One person who shall remain nameless (because I know the person in real life and don't want things to get weird) told me their consulting business was struggling and they wanted their blog critiqued.

Right off the bat I noticed a little button on his blog that said, "Buy me a coffee." It was linked to PayPal where you could send him a few bucks for whatever reason. It's no wonder his consulting business is struggling. This button on his blog is destroying any authority he's established. Nothing screams *not an expert* like a will-work-for-food sign.

Another example that goes right along with this but doesn't have a thing to do with blogging is the free lunch. You know what I'm talking about. Someone says, "I'd like to take you to lunch sometime and pick your brain." There's a lot wrong here. First of all, if you let someone buy your lunch in exchange for your expertise, you are showing them your expertise isn't worth much.

You're killing your authority for a cheeseburger and fries! Authorities don't trade their knowledge for a lunch. You shouldn't, either.

The second thing wrong here applies if you are the one asking someone to lunch. Unless you are a zombie, stop saying you want to "pick my brain"! It sounds disgusting and gross. I would like to nominate the phrase for abolishment from our language. If you tell someone you'd like to pick their brain, you deserve to be punched in the jeans.

Do not do things that diminish your credibility and authority. Be aware of your actions.

24

Shock and Awe

NEWS OUTLETS STILL HOLD A LOT OF POWER. People consume huge quantities of news each day. It plays too big a role to simply ignore, although most businesses do.

Generating publicity is typically hit or miss. It is very unpredictable. It's not a strategy I recommend spending a lot of time and energy on unless you've got some of the other strategies in this book nailed down.

The problem with buzz is that it doesn't last. (Insert your own "buzz doesn't last" joke here.) This is why you want to take advantage of any publicity you can get.

The good news is that generating publicity and buzz about your brand is a great way to grow your audience and your authority. When you're being quoted or written about in the media, you are establishing some powerful credibility. There are also a lot of opportunities out there to generate free publicity.

One of the reasons publicity works so well is that it's not seen as marketing. You're not shoving a marketing message in their face, so prospects don't feel as threatened. Many times the media comes across as a third-party endorsement.

Sadly, the reason most brands never receive any publicity is not because they aren't doing anything buzzworthy, although that doesn't help. It is because they don't get proactive in their attempts to generate publicity. Sitting around waiting for Matt Lauer to call you is not a good strategy. Plus, it sounds a little creepy.

It is up to you to take the first step. You must bring the story to the news outlets. Look, the media is constantly looking for something worthwhile to talk about. They are always interested in something newsworthy. Get to know reporters one on one.

You need to become a resource they can rely on. Become their industry expert in your field. If there is a news story that falls into your area of expertise and you don't reach out to add your two cents' worth, you are missing out on a huge opportunity.

> Never stop looking for an excuse to be in the media.

One of the best resources to find reporters who need some help is a site called HARO, or HelpAReporter.com. Every day they send out an e-mail with specific media queries. Find those you are qualified to be a source for and send them a simple, straight-to-the-point message. Make their job easier, and they will love you for it.

Understand that just because you reach out to the media doesn't mean they are going to put you on TV or on the cover of their magazine. They won't post or print it all. This is where the hit-or-miss element comes into play. Sometimes you've got something worth talking about and they run with it. Other times it's not what they are looking for. This is why you must work at it consistently while not becoming reliant on buzz and publicity alone.

When it comes to generating publicity, don't underestimate your local media. Regardless of where you live, the local media loves a "local guy or gal does good" story.

I once submitted a press release to a large newspaper in my town. Don't laugh! Newspapers were still relevant at this time and generated more business than you'd think. Anyway, my angle with the press release was about me being local, young, and doing business internationally.

There are a few things to take note of here. First off, thanks to the Internet, who isn't doing business internationally? Second, I wasn't exactly young. I was 28 or 29 at the time. This shows how much the media loves the local hero angle of a story.

The paper not only ran an article about my press release, but they put me on the front page of the business section. This increased my brand's visibility, increased my website traffic (for a day), and led to several new clients. Not bad for spending a few minutes e-mailing a press release.

Start small and work your way up.

I keep reminding you that publicity is hit or miss. Case in point: a friend of mine took a similar local hero angle for a press release about a product he was launching. In a nutshell, it was the same as mine. Did it get printed in his local paper? Nope. It was posted on the front page of Yahoo.com. The traffic he received was incredible, and he saw an immediate increase in sales.

Being shocking and controversial can certainly generate some publicity. Be careful that you are shocking and controversial in a way that appeals to your target audience. You want to be talked about in the media for the right reasons.

Is there such a thing as bad publicity? This question should never be asked. You better believe there is! This whole "any publicity is good publicity" nonsense is a bunch of crap.

If the media does a story on a hotel that has bed bugs and is infested with mice, is that good publicity? I mean after all, their brand is being talked about, right? I hope you see that the publicity is bad. Over time, people will forget the news story and start staying at the hotel again. But the hotel would certainly see a dip in business as a result of negative publicity.

Anything and everything that you have going on in your business can be newsworthy. New products or services you roll out could be newsworthy. Speaking at an event or putting on your own event could certainly be newsworthy. The ideas and options are endless. The thing is you just won't know until you try.

25

The Presentation Age

NEVER BEFORE HAD I THOUGHT of myself as a public speaker. After all, I had never done it before. But while attending a conference where I knew the organizer, I was asked if I could share what was working in my business to some of the attendees. I agreed for two reasons: first, because the organizer was a friend and I like helping my friends. And second, because I like attention. The farthest thing from my mind was that it would be great exposure for my personal brand.

He gave me all of four to five minutes to prepare. Then he opened the doors and walked on the stage to introduce me. I was shocked. This wasn't some small breakout session with 30 or 40 people like I was expecting. This was an audience of just over 2,000 people who were all looking at me like "who the heck is this guy?"

To say I was nervous would be a huge understatement. Completely freaked out is more like it. I went through all of the "tricks" to settle my nerves. None of them worked. Heck, I even pretended the audience was in their underwear, but there were a few unfortunate-looking people in the front row that gave me the creeps.

That was my first foray into public speaking. The moment it was over, I immediately knew I was hooked. I was hooked not only because of the attention but because it gave me instant credibility. After the session was finished, I was able to meet people face to face and have real conversations with them. I was able to get real feedback from them as well. Say what you will about the Internet, nothing beats a face-to-face connection.

Public speaking boosts your brand's visibility and establishes you as an authority in your field. I know the vast majority of people would rather poke their eyes out than speak in front of a group of people. That's exactly why public speaking is such a big opportunity. Your competition is scared to death as well.

When you can rise above your fears and give it a shot, you win. Let your competition stay home because they are afraid to do it. You don't have to start by speaking to a group of 2,000. Get your feet wet at a local meeting or gathering. Ease your way into it. Start small. You will get better with every presentation you do. A good friend of mine found speaking in front of people so frightening that he eased his way into it through teleseminars and webinars. He got used to presenting live and got comfortable with his content. Today, he is a very solid presenter.

There's no doubt my schoolteachers would be shocked to know I regularly get up and speak in front of people. In fact, most of my family still has a hard time believing it. When I was a kid I had a bad lisp. I was very self-conscious about it and had to go to speech therapy. Trust me when I say if I can do it, so can you.

Like anything when it comes to branding, you want to just be yourself when speaking. The audience wants to see you succeed. They certainly don't want to sit there and watch you awkwardly stumble through a presentation. That becomes uncomfortable for them as well. They want to be educated and entertained. One of the more common mistakes I see is when someone tries too hard to be perfect. Yes, you want to do well, but relax and have fun.

I rely on my content, passion, and energy when speaking. I'm not worried about being the most polished presenter on the planet, and you shouldn't be either. I've seen speakers about to go on stage reviewing a 17-point checklist they got at Toastmasters. They are frantically trying to remember every piece of advice they have been given. The only point I remind myself of is "Don't suck."

One of the worst mistakes you can make is to cram too much content into your presentation. I'm not saying the content shouldn't be good. It needs to be great. And your presentation should be heavy on the content. But by trying to cover too many points during your presentation, you will find yourself overwhelming the audience. How many key points can they possibly remember?

Any good presentation is full of stories. People remember stories. People share stories. Every time you make a point, you should have a great story to go with it. A great story reinforces what you are saying. The better storyteller you are, the better you'll be at public speaking.

Some speakers like to use slides; others do not. I can tell you that 99 percent of all slides are horrible. That's a true statistic that I just made up. The problem is people try to do too much with them. The vast majority of slide presentations have way too much text on each slide. I will often use nothing but pictures as my slides. The audience finds them far more interesting than trying to read a bunch of text. One last thing about slides: *please*, do *not* read your slides to the audience. It's safe to go ahead and assume they know how to read.

One of the most important parts of presenting, if not the most important, is the opening. You have to open strong. Open with a shocking statement or eye-opening statistic. Anything that will get the audience to sit up and pay attention. You want them to know your presentation is about to be different than the rest. Two of the most common openings I see are killing people's speaking careers. These are about the worst ways you can start a presentation. The first is with a joke. Jokes are extremely dangerous to open with. There's a good chance the audience won't find you as funny as you do. If you open with a joke and you hear crickets, then you're dead. The audience is uncomfortable and you will have lost your confidence right from the start. Let the humor come later in the presentation. The second mistake is to reintroduce yourself. Chances are the host of the event just introduced you and told the audience your name. The audience doesn't need you to repeat your name to them one more time.

Getting booked to speak somewhere is often a struggle for some. They aren't aware of upcoming events in their industry, and they don't have a network of people to contact. As with many things, the best way to get started is to keep it simple.

MeetUp.com is a site full of events big and small. The organizers of these events are often looking for someone to help fill the time with good content. They may not have a huge budget for you, and they may not have a dime to pay. But you have to start somewhere. Every successful speaker I know started by speaking anywhere they could for free.

The key is then to use your presentation as leverage for future gigs. *Always* get a video of you speaking. Share that video online and through social media. It not only builds your brand and lets people get more familiar with you, but it lets event organizers know you are a good speaker.

A friend of mine put on an event and asked several of his friends to speak at it. But one person was left out. When he asked why he wasn't included, the organizer of the event simply responded, "I didn't know you were a public speaker!" Don't let this happen to you. Make sure the world knows.

Public speaking increases the awareness of your brand to new audiences and allows you the chance to build relationships with peers inside your industry. Some of my strongest allies in business I met because we were both speakers at the same event. You will not only increase your brand awareness and credibility. You will also increase sales. Whether you are getting paid a flat fee to speak or are selling products in the back of the room, public speaking is too big of an opportunity to neglect.

26

Video Made the Internet Star

VIDEO MAY HAVE KILLED THE RADIO STAR, but it created the Internet star. Using video in your marketing is without a doubt one of the most effective ways to build your brand and increase your online presence.

Today's world has grown up with video. We're conditioned to watch it. We're conditioned to share it. There's an endless number of ways to use video in your business. You just have to decide which approach is best for you.

Video has high perceived value and allows your audience to get to know you better because they get to see your personality in action. Video is also extremely easy for your audience to share. It's also pretty easy for you to make.

You don't need a fancy studio with lights and props to make a great video. It can be as simple as recording the video on your cell phone and uploading it to the Internet in a matter of seconds. Here are a few ideas on using video in your marketing that you can implement right away:

- Video testimonials: I touch on this later in Chapter 28. A testimonial captured on video is one of the ultimate forms of proof. A great way to get some testimonials on video would be to offer people something of value for doing it. I once held a video testimonial contest. I had clients film a video testimonial on their own and upload it to YouTube. The client who submitted the best and most original testimonial would win free admission into my coaching program for the next year. The best part? I got a bunch of great testimonials on video that I can use whenever I see fit.

- Video content: Obviously video is a great method of showcasing your content. If you're too shy to be in front of the camera, you can record a slideshow video of your content using tools such as Camtasia or Screen Flow. You will be heard, but instead of seeing you on the video, your audience will see a Keynote or PowerPoint presentation of your slides.

- Public speaking: Always be sure to film your presentation when speaking at an event. It's great content where your audience can see you in action. Just look at how popular the TED Talks videos are. Their videos are short and packed full of great content. People love them and they love to share them.

- Videos in uncommon places: Think outside of the box and go beyond the typical content or sales video. Put a video on your thank you pages on your website that people can view after they've made a purchase. Seeing you thank them is more powerful than some basic copy that says, "Thanks! We're processing your order" like more sites say.

  Another uncommon place to use video is the FAQ page on your site. Frequently asked questions can get pretty dull. Why not spice things up a bit by answering the questions in a video? You get to showcase your personality and have some fun with it at the same time.

- Video of you in action: That doesn't sound right, does it? Get your head out of the gutter. What I mean is using video to show exactly how your product or service works. Graco is one of the largest brands in the world of baby and infant products. They know how to make good use of video. While shopping for a baby swing when my wife and I were expecting our first child, we came across a really cool swing made by Graco. It was the Graco Sweetpeace Infant Soothing Swing, to be exact. They could have come up with a better name, but that's beside the point. The swing does a lot of unique stuff, and you can even hook your iPod up to it so that your new baby can rock out to some Green Day while they nap. Graco knows they've got a good product in this swing, but they also know that the best way to sell us on all of the nifty things it does is to show us. They created a great video showing the swing in action. The video answers just about every question you'd have about the swing. There's no doubt they sell more of them because of it.

One of the main reasons people don't visit a new church is because they don't know what to expect. They don't know which doors to go in. They don't know how to dress. People are always afraid of looking stupid. A church could ease these fears by posting a simple video on their website with a tour of the church and what to do and where to go, starting from when they pull into the parking lot. Video can take the unknown element out of the equation for prospects.

As you can see, video works in any industry. The sky is the limit on how many ways you can use it in your business. It doesn't even have to be recorded video to work! From time to time I broadcast a live feed on the Internet through a service such as Ustream. My audience can watch me live, online, answering their questions and ranting about who knows what. It's a great chance for them to see me and get to know my personality. It's nonthreatening for them. Plus, sometimes I give away some cool stuff, and who doesn't love free cool stuff?

Being on camera makes a lot of people nervous. I get it. We all hate the sound of our own voice and the camera adds 10 pounds, so it must be evil. But don't let those fears keep you from making awesome videos. They don't have to be perfect. In fact, statistics show that people prefer a raw video over a polished one. They like to see that you are real. Mistakes make you human, so don't sweat them. I have a two-take policy in my business. If I screw up the first take, then no matter what happens on take two, we're shipping it.

You're not Stephen Spielberg. Quit trying to make your videos perfect.

Video is the most effective way to become real in the eyes of your prospects. It's a tool that rivals social media in terms of effectiveness. You're missing a huge opportunity if you're not using video to promote your brand. Make them fun and real. Just make them.

27

Brand Alliance

WHAT'S BETTER THAN WORKING HARD to promote your brand and making sales as a result? Having other people promote your brand and making sales. Having affiliates who promote your product or service to their own audience and community is one of the quickest ways to grow your brand and business.

Most people are aware of what an affiliate is, but just in case you don't, an affiliate is simply someone who promotes your products or services in exchange for a commission. They share the same audience as you but offer that audience something different. For example, someone who shares my audience of entrepreneurs and business owners but teaches them time management skills, rather than branding, would make a good affiliate.

Aligning yourself and partnering with other people of influence is a great strategy for your brand. If you sell sports hats, wouldn't it make sense to have people who sell shirts or jerseys of sports to be an affiliate of yours? Of course it would.

So how do you get affiliates and motivate them to promote you? It's actually easier than you think.

Affiliates aren't that much different than your customers. You have to build a relationship with them first and foremost. Second, you have to let them know what's in it for them. Sure you're paying them a commission, but there's more to it than that. They also want to know that their audience will benefit from your product or service and know that their audience will appreciate that they informed them of your product or service.

Take your time establishing a relationship with them. Don't ask them to promote you the first time you meet. That's like proposing on the first date. Ask them how you can be of help to them. Be genuine about the relationship, and don't expect anything in return. In other words, don't become friends with someone just because you want them to promote your stuff. Not all of them will, and that's okay.

Potential affiliates are everywhere. You don't have to search high and low to find them. Some of the best places to meet potential affiliates are at industry events. That's right, I'm talking about good old-fashioned face-to-face interactions. Every now and then it's okay to step away from the computer and do something offline. Conferences are full of people in the same industry as you or who at least share the same passion as you.

You can also find potential affiliates when you are a speaker at an event. Some of my most successful affiliates are people who I met while we were speaking at an event. Again, we met in real life first and built a relationship. Don't ask them to be an affiliate when you just met.

Another great way to find affiliates is through social media. In fact, six of my top-10 affiliates I met through social media. We spent months talking online and building the relationship. Over a period of time we would connect via other methods such as e-mail and the phone. Remember the phone? Apparently people still use it.

A very powerful way to find affiliates, who will gladly promote you, is to turn to your happy customers. They've used your product or service and like it. It only makes sense to reward them for helping you spread the word.

Ryan Allis is the CEO of iContact, a company that provides e-mail marketing solutions to businesses. Once while talking to Ryan I asked him about how he grew the company from the ground up. There was a lot Ryan and his team did, but he mentioned to me that their affiliate program really helped things take off. iContact focused on their customers with their affiliate program. Turning your customers into affiliates can really boost sales.

When you have a relationship and friendship with someone, it makes sense they would support you and vice versa. In fact, one of the best ways to get someone to be an affiliate of yours is for you to promote them to your audience first. Again, don't do it for the sole reason of hoping they return the favor, because they are under no obligation to do so.

Because affiliate marketing also involves you promoting someone else's product or service, I have to urge you to be careful about who you choose to promote. Every affiliate affects your brand and reputation. Do not let someone of questionable character align with your brand. You don't want affiliates who spam people because it reflects badly on you.

Also, don't shove affiliate promotions down your audience's throat. Yes, it's awesome that you make a commission for selling a product that you didn't create. That doesn't mean your audience wants to see a new offer every day of the week.

Getting affiliates and having them be happy to promote you consistently is all about the relationship. Just like we do business with people we know, like, and trust, we also promote people we know, like, and trust. Treat your affiliates as great as you would a customer. Stay in touch with them often and maintain the relationship. They will provide a big boost for your brand and business.

28

Dirty Little Secret

THERE IS A SECRET WEAPON floating around the marketing world that really isn't a secret at all. Yet for some reason, it is one of the most underused and overlooked weapons in all of marketing. When used properly, it will add credibility to your brand and make your selling process 10 bazillion times easier (actual number).

Establishing credibility is one of the most important aspects of branding and positioning yourself as an authority in your field. This little secret is hands down, without a doubt, my favorite weapon to use to establish credibility.

Of course, I'm talking about testimonials.

Testimonials are, by far, the most underused element in all of marketing. This is the case for two reasons. First, most businesses don't know how to collect them. Second, most businesses don't know what to do with them when they get them.

Testimonials are so powerful because people will believe what others are saying about you over what you say about yourself. Of course you and your mom think you are awesome. We want to know what people who have actually done business with you think. Social proof is critical and cannot be underestimated.

Testimonials let your fans say what you cannot.

You must be collecting testimonials and using them in all of your marketing efforts. They should be front and center in all you do.

Having a page on your website with nothing but testimonials is great, except that no one is looking at that page. *No one* clicks that "see what our clients are saying" link. Don't hide them or bury them on some page within your website. Don't make people search for them. They need to be on your home page. They need to be throughout your sales presentation. They need to be on your direct mail pieces. They need to be everywhere.

Testimonials will increase sales and provide you with the credibility that shows people you know what you are doing. Never stop collecting testimonials. There's no such thing as too many when it comes to testimonials. If you have two or three prospects, chalk that up to you got lucky. If you have 30, then now you are getting somewhere.

A recent trend I have noticed has me greatly annoyed with some marketers out there. This trend is using testimonials that aren't believable. I am not talking about testimonials that seem too good to be true. I am talking about testimonials with no name, no photo, or anything else that would prove the person is real and that they actually said something nice about you.

Damage can be done to your brand when your testimonials are not believable. If I see a testimonial with no name attached to it, I can only assume you made it up. If the person truly said it, then he or she is fine with their name being used. These days a lot of smart marketers are collecting video testimonials, which is the ultimate proof.

However, even video testimonials have to be looked at closely. There are websites out there where for just $5 you can get someone to record a video testimonial for you. You write the script, and they send you the video. This is a frightening situation if you ask me.

Do what you can to prove that your testimonials are the real deal. First, always include the person's name. Preferably their first name *and* last name. Second, include a photo of the person (with their permission). Also, include other facts about them such as their website address, occupation, or location.

As I mentioned before, the ultimate testimonial is a video testimonial. Whenever possible, ask your customers for one. I once knew a real estate agent who would send prospects a DVD full of video testimonials. By the time he arrived at their home for his presentation, they were already sold.

When I'm speaking at events I often include testimonials or case studies as part of my presentation. When I do this I also share the person's Twitter ID so people can write to them and verify they are a real person and verify that they are, in fact, a fan. I also try to collect video testimonials whenever possible.

Collecting testimonials is easy, assuming your product or service actually does what it promises to do. But you should have a strategy and a system for collecting testimonials on a regular basis. The easiest way I know of to obtain a testimonial is to—drum roll, please—*ask for them*. Pretty simple.

When you do a good job and have satisfied clients, you will receive e-mails, social media feedback, and even good old-fashioned handwritten notes that are full of glowing testimonials. Use them in *all* of your marketing. A satisfied client is always happy to say a kind word about you.

29

Little Things

LITTLE THINGS MATTER. A lot. Every single interaction someone has with you and your company has an effect on your brand, and that effect is either positive or negative. There is no in-between. You must strive to make each experience a positive one and one that they will remember.

I'm often called in by brands to find areas to enhance customer experience. What I see is that most businesses fail to maximize on their brand touch points. A touch point is simply any form of contact someone has with your brand. It can be an e-mail, conversation with an employee, direct mail piece, commercial, or blog post. Understand that every touch point counts, no matter if it's big or small.

Remember that your brand is always on display. All the little things count, and it's your job to be sure they leave a positive opinion of the brand you've created.

This means that every employee is a brand ambassador of your business. The sooner you accept that, the better. Oftentimes a single bad experience with an employee will cause a customer to be lost forever.

Have you ever been to a restaurant where the food was great but the server was rude? It happens far too often, and it makes it super easy for those customers to start going to the restaurant across the street.

> The best brands not only deliver a solid product or service, they deliver an incredible experience.

The good news is that interactions with employees can also leave a very positive effect on your brand. My wife and I went to Hobby Lobby to get a few custom picture frames made. I'll admit Hobby Lobby isn't my favorite place in the world, but I'm just not as into arts and crafts as my wife is. So I was dreading how long getting these frames might take and feared becoming bored to death.

Much to my surprise the experience was nothing like I expected. The gentleman helping us was named Claudio, and his family had been building frames for generations. He was so passionate about his work that it was inspiring. He moved like lightning and told us stories of his family making frames in Europe many years ago. I only wish everyone approached their job with such passion.

The experience was great not only because we got the frames we needed, but also because this employee single-handedly made it fun and engaging. We could have gone to several other places to get the frames made, but would the experience have been the same? Doubtful. It truly is the little things that count.

Even having a one-on-one conversation with someone is a brand experience for that person. If you think it's okay to get hammered at a hotel bar with friends because you're "off the clock," think again. You're never off the clock when it comes to your brand.

Every moment in front of a customer is a golden opportunity. Michael Eisner, former CEO of Disney, once said, "A brand is a living entity—and it is enriched or undermined cumulatively over time, the product of a thousand small gestures." These small touch points matter more than you know. They determine your brand value.

It should come as no surprise when I tell you that I hate the dentist. It's not me, it's him. I'm assuming you feel the same way because going to the dentist is scary. I know Randal Garner feels that way and he *is* a dentist! That's what motivated him to start Dental Bliss.

You see, like all of us, Randal was afraid of the dentist. So, he became one. Doesn't seem to make sense until you learn what he has created with Dental Bliss. His dental practice offers an experience like no other. The experience he has created begins when you first walk in the door. First off, it looks like a spa, not a dentist office. Second, Randal has implemented the latest technology to make your experience awesome. They don't use drills, shots, or anything that will make you bleed. It's all done with laser technology and is completely pain free. It's so amazing there, it almost makes you wish you had a toothache!

Randal has made sure Dental Bliss offers a unique experience by focusing on the little things. He wants his customers to be wowed before, during, and after their experience at Dental Bliss.

But touch points don't stop when a sale is made. Once you've made a sale, the opportunity to create a brand advocate begins.

What do you do when someone purchases your product or service? Once you are done celebrating, do you follow up with them? I'm going to go out on a limb and guess that you don't. But you should! Your product may be amazing, but that doesn't mean your customer will know how to use it properly or get the most out of it. A simple follow-up phone call or e-mail can go a *long* way toward strengthening the relationship with your customers.

People often associate their feelings and opinions about a brand with the way they buy the product. Regardless of what kind of product or service you sell, you are selling an experience. That experience should be easy, fun, and remarkable. It should be worth talking about.

Once someone makes a purchase they are a bazillion times more likely to purchase from you again. Don't be "one and done" when it comes to sales. You're trying to build a stable business, and you do that with repeat customers. Take care of them and help them get the most out of what you have to offer. The better the results they get and the more satisfied they are, the more likely they are to spread the word about what you do.

A close examination of great businesses and brands will reveal they are mastering the little things. They are not only going above and beyond with the big things, but they are putting the spotlight on each and every interaction a customer has with them. Little things add up to big things. It's not going to be one single thing you do that makes your brand a success. It's going to be the thousands of little things you do right.

30

Race to the Bottom

THE PRICE OF YOUR PRODUCTS or services can be an excellent way to position your brand. Your price helps dictate how prospects perceive the value you offer through your product or service. Being the lowest priced option will give people one feeling about your brand; a higher price will give them another. What customers expect from you is often determined by price. The old saying "You get what you pay for" is a cliché for a reason. People truly believe they get what they pay for. Is your brand a premium, higher option or is it a type of commodity, lower option?

Being the highest price in the marketplace may not be the positioning you want. You don't have to have an exclusive or luxury brand to have success. That being said, being the lowest price is a position I would never recommend. Ever. Low pricing is a race to the bottom of the marketplace.

One of the problems with trying to be the cheapest price is that it is far too easy for someone to come along and price their product or service lower than yours. If you think having the lowest price in your industry is a good strategy, remember that someone is always willing to go broke faster than you. Someone will go cheaper than you, even if it puts them out of business.

Low price positioning means your business might as well be standing on quicksand. There is no loyalty for brands positioned on the low end of price. The customer will go to who is offering the lowest price. At what point do you stop lowering your prices? You can only go so low on price. Most keep lowering them until they are out of business.

All of your hard work and effort toward becoming an expert and authority in your field are wasted if you are the lowest price. Would you choose a heart surgeon based on who was the cheapest or based on who was the best? You would want to use the most credible expert you could find. Often a "bargain" price takes away the idea that you are an authority.

This is one of several reasons I turn down offers like "Can I buy you lunch and pick your brain?" First off, stop saying you want to "pick my brain." That is disgusting, gross, and doesn't sound like a lot of fun for me. Second, if I'm willing to give out my advice and expertise for free food, how much of an expert could I really be? The other issue is perceived value. If someone gets some good advice and it only cost them a lunch, then where is the motivation to implement any of the ideas? When someone has no skin in the game, they are far less likely to take action. If they paid me $10,000 to go to lunch with them, they would take action on every idea they received to get a good return on investment. (On a side note, if you'd like to pay me $10,000 to go to lunch, you just name the place!)

Being a premium-priced brand means that your business is on more solid footing. A premium brand can afford to do more for their customers. You can provide a better service for your customers and do things for them that your lower priced competitors cannot. You can provide a lot more value to people. Customer retention is much higher for premium and exclusive brands.

Your price attracts or repels a certain kind of customer. When you know who your ideal client is, you will know if your price is attractive to them or not. A higher price most likely means fewer customers, but that isn't a bad thing. If you are making more per customer due to your price, then you don't need as many customers to hit your goals. You can focus on serving the number of customers that you can easily handle.

The people who regularly make a purchase based on price alone are the people who have to. According to some statistics this is less than

10 percent of the marketplace. Do you want to market to people with money or those without it? If a customer only does business with you because you're a steal of a deal, then they will leave you the moment they find it cheaper somewhere else.

Running a sale is not as good an idea as it may seem upfront. The customers who take you up on a sale are the customers who are already loyal to your brand. They would buy from you anyway. They appreciate the sale because they know what your normal prices are. In my opinion, all a sale does is show people you were priced too high to begin with. Sell at low prices and you will train and condition your audience to expect low prices from you.

People rarely buy your brand for the first time because of a slash in price. Keep in mind that you should never compete based on price. When I see a marketing campaign that is focused on price only it scares me. I want to know that a company has more to offer me than a low price. I want to know the benefits of the product or service. Too many businesses compete on price when they should be competing on value.

> The price isn't too low, the value is.

Price often gets the blame when a product fails. Although price could certainly be the culprit, most of the time it is not. The problem is that consumers failed to see the value in it. When selling your product or service, focus on value, not price.

> Price is only an issue to prospects when they cannot see the value in your offer.

If we see the value, then we will happily pay. If you want to charge more, no problem. Just make sure you add more value for us. This ties into showing us the benefits of your product or service. If we see what's in it for us, and we see that it will add value to our lives, then we're all in. If you leave us searching for the value, then we'll leave you searching for the sale.

31

Longing to Belong

Do you remember all those silly high school cliques, the ones we were desperate to be a part of and made life horrible when they wouldn't let us in? That need to belong has been instilled in all of us since a very early age. We all want to feel like we are a part of something. Everyone wants to feel like they belong.

There's not a person on earth who isn't looking for their place. That place where it's okay to be yourself because you are with others just like you. I've always felt like being an entrepreneur is very lonely, so when I find myself surrounded by other like-minded entrepreneurs, I feel at home. We're on the same page. We can talk about the same things. There's an understanding and connection with each other based on our commonality, even if the rest of our lives are at polar opposite ends of the spectrum.

Your fans, audience, or whatever you want to call them, all have that longing to belong. They want to be a part of something that is fun, exciting, and has a real sense of community. Have you ever noticed how motorcycle drivers almost always wave at other motorcycle drivers or how drivers notice others with the same make and model of car? They don't even know each other, yet there is a connection. That connection is based on the commonality and significance of liking the same thing.

111

Harley Davidson has an enormous number of fans. Not only are these fans super passionate, but they also *want* to hang around with other Harley Davidson fans. They organize their own events and trips that all evolve around one common factor: They are all Harley Davidson fans.

Am I saying you want to establish a cult-like following? Yes and no. If by "cult" you mean a passionate fan base and a strong following, then the answer is most definitely "Yes." If by "cult" you mean people getting together to wear creepy robes, drink blood, and/or paint satanic images on the floor, then the answer is a resounding "Hell, no."

You want to align yourself with your audience and create a strong feeling of "us." People should feel a bond with you like they are a part of something bigger than just themselves.

When your audience sees that you share the same values as they do, you begin to build a level of trust with them.

Nothing creates a stronger bond than an "us versus them" mentality. You want to create a feeling that they are part of a larger "us." Position your brand and its fans as being against "them." I'm doing it with you in this book, right now. Those of us who "brand against the machine" do things differently. We're fed up with the boring ways businesses market themselves.

We are the cool people. "They" are not. ☺

One great way to establish this sense of community is to give your fans and followers a name. A name gives them an identity and separation from the status quo that increases a sense of community and the feeling of belonging.

Let's look at a few examples. One of the most popular examples of naming your fans is from the band The Grateful Dead. The people in their passionate fan base are known as Deadheads. Deadheads even invented their own language and slang. You know a fellow Deadhead by the language they use. Creating a language that only you and your fans use builds a super tight bond that is very hard to break. Even former President Bill Clinton and legendary basketball coach Phil Jackson are Deadheads.

Jimmy Buffet fans are known as Parrotheads. Fans of pop singer Lady Gaga are known as her Little Monsters. (To show her dedication to her fans, Lady Gaga even got "Little Monsters" tattooed on her arm.) One of my favorite rock bands, Better Than Ezra, affectionately refers to their fans as Ezralites. And finally, the hit TV show *Mad Men* certainly has a loyal fan base. They are known as Maddicts, and I'm proud to say I'm one of them. I love that show.

Members of my community are known as Outcasts because they are going against what is normal and common. As a reader of this book I now consider you an Outcast. Welcome to the club!

When a community has a name, it becomes easier and more natural for them to refer to themselves as such and to talk about it to other people. It allows people to feel like they are a part of something important. You're either in or you're out. You are either cool or you are lame. There is no in-between.

People love to be a part of a movement, so why aren't you creating a sense of belonging with your audience? Why not let them be a part of your own movement?

32

Brand Without a Cause

ARE YOU A BRAND without a cause? Sure, you're in business to make money, provide value, and all that jazz. But does your business align with a cause that helps those in need? If it does, then good for you! If it doesn't, then you may want to seriously consider it.

Make no mistake about it: giving to charity is a good marketing strategy. And there is nothing wrong with that. It's not about greed. It's about the numerous benefits of using your brand to help others. If there's a charity that speaks to your heart and you are in a position to give back, then I feel it's your obligation. You'll often see marketing offers mention that a certain percentage of sales are going to a charity. This is a win-win-win.

The customers win because they get the product/service they want and they can feel good about themselves for helping someone in need. The charity wins because it is getting donations and attention it wouldn't have had otherwise. And you win because it's showing the community that you care. And when you can involve your customers in giving back, you'll build a super tight relationship with them.

Some studies have shown that more than 80 percent of Americans think positively of brands that support a charity or cause that they are passionate about. Almost 70 percent have said they would pay more for a product if it is associated with a cause/charity that they care about. This means if all things are equal, price, quality, and so on, that consumers will choose the business that is aligned with their passion and motivation for helping a worthy cause.

Blake Mycoskie started his business TOMS Shoes with the purpose of being able to help others. For every pair of TOMS shoes you purchase, the company gives a pair of new shoes to a child in need. This is a perfect example of a strong brand using charity in a way that really helps others. When you buy a pair of their shoes, you get a cool pair of new shoes, plus you feel good about yourself for helping someone you will never meet. These children are helped because they live in a country where they do not have the same opportunities that you and I have. In many cases it is the child's very first pair of shoes. Finally, TOMS wins because they make a sale, and, more importantly, they make a difference.

By building a strong, visible brand, you create the opportunity to use that visibility and influence to help causes you are passionate about. You put yourself in a better position to help others in times of need.

When I was in real estate, the brokerage I was partnered with got involved with Relay for Life. I've personally lost a lot of family members to cancer and the American Cancer Society is a great organization, so it was an easy decision to get involved with Relay for Life. The idea was for every agent in the office to raise enough money to hit the goal we had set. My competitive spirit got to me, and I started running my mouth about how I could raise more money than the rest of the office combined. Our office had about 40 real estate agents at the time, so it wasn't going to be a walk in the park. But I knew I had a large community of people who were familiar with my brand and with whom I had good strong relationships. I simply sent everyone an e-mail explaining that I was raising money for this great cause I was very passionate about. It didn't matter if the donation was big or small because every little bit made a difference. When things were all said and done, I raised about $200 more than the entire office of 40 agents combined.

Most of the real estate agents asked their close family and friends for donations, but I was able to ask a much larger audience of people who were familiar with me. During the process I also heard several heartbreaking stories from my audience about the loved ones they had lost to cancer. There were also more than a handful of people who shared with me their story of kicking cancer's ass. I felt more connected with my audience than ever before. I had used my relationships with those who felt connected to my brand to help support a cause I cared about. Everyone wins in this situation.

What I did was nothing new by any stretch of the imagination. We've witnessed celebrities leverage their personal brands to raise money and awareness for great causes for years. Whether it's Hurricane Katrina or the devastating earthquake then tsunami that hit Haiti, we've seen celebrities use their brand to help others. In 2010 a major flood hit my hometown of Nashville. Flooding in Nashville is so rare; many called it a 500-year flood. During this time the national news media wasn't giving the story much attention, despite the fact that lives were lost and damages amounted to over $1 billion. As the home of country music it was no surprise that a bunch of country music stars in Nashville came together to raise money. But what was a surprise was how Nashvillians used social media to reach out to their audiences and help raise money through the Red Cross. Every time someone reached out to their online following, their following responded by sharing the news with their own following. A major snowball effect was started, and a lot of money was raised to help those who had literally lost everything.

Frank McKinney is a daredevil entrepreneur and best-selling author. Frank has had success in several areas, but what drives him the most is his Caring House Project Foundation. Through the foundation Frank does a lot of work to help provide housing, food, and water for the homeless around the world.

Last year, I had the honor and privilege to donate some of my products and services to an auction that Frank held at a conference where we were both speaking. My items in the auction raised enough money to build a home for a family of eight in Haiti. That's a feeling that never gets old.

It is moments like these that I hope define my career. When you can use your brand and influence to help others, I believe you should.

Building a strong following for your brand is the key to business success. But it doesn't stop there. It puts you in a position to be able to make a difference in times that really matter. Sadly, a lot of businesses and high-profile personal brands choose not to align with charities that speak to them. Maybe they weren't hugged enough as a kid or something. Don't be one of those people. If you can call on the relationships you've created with your community to help those who are in desperate need, then please do. Everyone will be better for it.

33

Why Your Website Sucks

IF YOU THINK your website is perfect, then you need this chapter more than you know. Most of the websites floating around cyberspace are not doing their job. Most of them are ineffective. Chalk this up to approach, design, or whatever you want. The reality is that most of your thoughts on websites are wrong.

Your website, any website actually, has but one goal. That goal is to turn strangers into prospects and turn prospects into customers. That's it. There is no other goal.

> If your website doesn't have a function or generate leads, it's just a fancy brochure.

This is where most brands get it wrong. Their website looks like an online business card. There's no headline or call to action. There's no lead generation method. It's just a display page that provides no real value and doesn't tell the brand story well.

You want your website visitors to do one of three things when they land on your site:

1. Give you permission to follow up with them.

2. Buy something.
3. Share it with a friend or social network.

There is nothing more and nothing less than these three desired outcomes. Anything else you are attempting to accomplish is a waste of time, energy, and effort. Your website should start a conversation. That conversation could be with you, or it could be with a friend they are sharing the site with. Most of the time that conversation is with themselves as they evaluate if you have the solution they are looking for.

Your website, like any piece of marketing, should have a strong, attention-grabbing headline. You literally have just a few seconds before someone makes up their mind about staying on your site or clicking away to something else. Have a headline that stops them dead in their tracks and forces them to take notice. Let them know they've found what they are looking for.

Google.com is one of the most popular websites of all time, if not the most popular. Why does it work so well? Simplicity. It isn't giving you hundreds of options. It is giving you two. Search for something or leave. Most websites offer way too many choices for their visitors to think about. Before you pay someone thousands of dollars for some fancy-pants website design with all the bells and whistles, think of Google. Think of the simplicity. The first second it appears too busy and is overwhelming to them, people will leave. Simple works.

Your website should be about getting people to the next step you want them to take: moving them through your funnel and providing value to them every step of the way. If you are attempting to accomplish something more than that, you are wasting opportunity.

Many times your website will be the first point of contact someone has with your brand. What kind of impression will it make? Will it make them want to take the next logical step and view you as a solution to their problem? It had better. Everything else is just a waste.

34

Misunderstood

A LOT OF PEOPLE SAY e-mail marketing is dead. We'll refer to those people as idiots. E-mail marketing is not dead. Most people are just doing it wrong. It is still one of the most effective methods of communicating with your audience. If you're not building a healthy list of e-mail subscribers, you are leaving a lot of money on the table.

Let me be perfectly clear that I am not talking about spamming people. If every e-mail you send to your subscribers is a sales promotion, you are doing it wrong. Very wrong. E-mail is an excellent avenue to get your content to those who are looking forward to it.

Sure, you can promote your products and services to your e-mail subscribers and you should. But if that's the only thing you do, you're going to be one of those people who think e-mail is dead. Remember what we call them?

Let's go over each element of an effective e-mail so you can start to use this formula in your marketing today.

The most important part of any e-mail is the subject line. Your subject line is basically like a headline. It's one of the biggest determining factors in whether or not someone will open your e-mail. If your e-mails don't get opened, they don't get read. If they don't get read, then they can't read your content or promotional offer. This means you don't make money, and that's not cool.

I spend more time writing the subject line than I do the body of the e-mail. It's that important. You want a subject line that will not only get attention but one that will also invoke enough curiosity to get them to open the e-mail. Curiosity is a strong weapon in terms of copy. Here are some of my most successful e-mail subject lines:

I quit

I just hooked you up

Do not do this

My big mistake

The most underused weapon in marketing

A very useful resource

Notice they are fairly short and very conversational. They aren't boring subject lines like "Issue 23: The Success Issue" or "50% off all in-stock shoes." People's inboxes are crowded. Subject lines like that are easy to ignore and click Delete. I've found the shorter the subject line, the better, because so many people today are checking their e-mail on their phone.

You actually want to keep the entire copy of your e-mails very conversational. Tell a story. An e-mail with fancy pictures and little copy doesn't entice someone to click the link you want them to click.

The very first sentence in your e-mail also determines whether or not they will open it. A lot of e-mail programs display a preview of the first sentence of an e-mail. Your first sentence should reinforce the subject line and remain conversational.

It always drives me crazy to get an e-mail that says "Dear John" or "Dear valued subscriber." No one I know and like sends me e-mails like that. Write copy like it came from a friend. If I e-mail my brother, I don't start it with "Dear Jason." I either skip the greeting and get right to the point or I say something like "hey dude" or just "hey." Your e-mails need to feel like they are coming from a friend.

The last element that plays a factor in getting your e-mails opened is who it's from. People like doing business with people. Your e-mails should come from you, not ABC Realty. If I get an e-mail from a company, it's the last e-mail I open if I even open it at all. Typically I just delete it because I know it's a sales pitch that I don't have time for.

The body of your e-mail should tell a story as I mentioned earlier. It should be entertaining and easy to read. People are too busy and have too much e-mail to read your professional manuscript. Just write how you talk.

Let's talk about the number one mistake people make in their e-mails. That mistake is trying to sell in the e-mail. Your e-mail marketing will never be successful if you try to sell in the e-mail itself. Instead you want to link to a website that does the selling. Your e-mail should only sell them on clicking the link. That's it.

The end of your e-mail should include a P.S. It seems kind of silly, but the P.S. is the most read part of an e-mail. Use the P.S. to summarize what the e-mail was about and what step you want them to take next.

E-mail is a great way to get your content to your audience and to build that relationship. You don't want to overwhelm someone by e-mailing them every single day, but you also don't want to wait too long between e-mails. The longer you wait between e-mails, the easier it is for you to get lost in the mix. How much is too much? That answer depends on your audience, and it's something you'll want to test. That being said, never forget there is no such thing as too much follow-up.

I'd rather have someone unsubscribe from my e-mail list because I sent them too many e-mails than to lose sales and relationships with people because I failed to stay in touch with them.

The time of day and day of the week you send your e-mails will factor greatly into their success. Sending an e-mail at 10 P.M. on a Wednesday night probably isn't a good idea. That being said, there's no real magic day and time. I can tell you that my audience is most responsive to e-mails that are sent in the morning and during the middle of the week. It's something you'll want to test and see how your audience responds. You may find that you get good results on weekends when most do not.

One thing about e-mail marketing that I want you to really grasp is the monitoring of unsubscribers. Don't do it. Every time you send an e-mail out, people are going to unsubscribe. Paying attention to that number is only going to depress you and throw you off your game.

When someone unsubscribes from my list, I'm glad. They weren't going to buy from me anyway, so why have them waste space?

When people become fans of your brand, they'll actually look forward to your e-mails. They will especially look forward to them assuming you are providing them with awesome content that is useful to them. Don't underestimate e-mail marketing. It's one of the best ways to build a relationship with your audience.

35

The Hangout

I HAVE A CONFESSION to make to you. When I first heard about Facebook I thought it was the dumbest thing that had come from the Internet since Al Gore invented it. A friend told me about it and described it to me as a cool place to reconnect with people I went to high school with. I hated the people I went to high school with. Why on earth would I want to reconnect with them today?

I admit I was wrong to judge it so early. Facebook has become a force to be reckoned with. Heck, 600 million people can't be wrong, right? Of those 600 million people there's a pretty darn good chance your audience is in there somewhere. Your brand must have a presence there.

As your brand grows, people will want to connect with you on Facebook. Most will start by sending you a friend request. That's great except that Facebook limits the number of friends you have to 5,000. The good news is there is no limit to the number of people that can connect with you on your fan page.

As I mentioned in Chapter 17, "Welcome to the Social Parade," social media is all about engagement. If every post on your fan page is news or a promotion, you are doing it wrong. You want it to be a place where people can interact with you.

A hundred fully engaged fans are better than a thousand unengaged fans.

Be informal with your updates and conversations. That's why people are there. No one uses Facebook to have promotions pushed on them. Remember that people don't care about your business; they care about themselves. Mix it up and have some fun. Give them a reason to be there. Share insider tips, industry and company news, and run some fun contests.

Speaking of contests, they work very well if and only if people feel like they stand a shot to win. I cringe whenever I see a brand running a contest on their fan page that goes something like this:

"Come like us on Facebook! We're giving away a free iPad to our 1,000th fan!"

This looks okay on the surface. But typically they run this contest when they are a few fans out from a thousand. So if you go to their fan page and see they have 982 fans, you're not going to "like" their page. Why would you? You know you won't be the one getting the iPad. Create a contest that is fun, easy, and believable that people stand a chance at winning.

Keep your page from becoming static. Update at least three times per week. Those updates can be a variation of posts, videos, handling customer support, or sharing photos. I like to mix in photos and videos as frequently as possible so my fans don't become bored with basic updates.

The biggest problem with most fan pages is that there is no interaction between the brand and the fans. Hands down the best way to get a conversation going is to ask questions. Everyone loves to give you their two cents on something. Let's see just how effective asking questions are.

These are three different status updates from Oreo's fan page. Can you guess which one resulted in the most interaction?

1. The new Double Stuf OREO SONIC Blast coming to Sonic Drive-In next month is OREO Creme flavored real ice cream

blended and topped with crunchy OREO pieces. It's not just fun to eat . . . it's a Blast!
2. How would you describe Oreo cookies to someone who has never tasted them?
3. An Oreo cookie tastes like . . .

Status 1 resulted in 1,945 Likes and 202 Comments. Not too shabby. Status 2, which is a question, resulted in 4,553 Likes and 3,641 Comments. That's a big difference from status 1. And our winner is status 3. It's a short, simple fun question that resulted in 8,487 Likes and 6,605 Comments.

As you can see, a question gets conversations started. Once a conversation is started, you can begin to engage with your fans and keep that conversation going. Posting a question generates more comments, and the more people who comment on your status the more often you show up on people's newsfeed in Facebook. Oreo also does a "fan of the week," which is a lot of fun and people respond to it very well. Oreo does a phenomenal job on its fan page and is one of the best brands on Facebook in my opinion. They also happen to make one heck of a cookie.

> They call it a "fan page" for a reason: It's not about you—it's about your fans.

The more you can put the attention on them the better. You can do a "fan of the week" like Oreo does or have them post photos of them using your product (assuming your product is something that is appropriate for public viewing). I am always flattered when meeting someone in person at an event or wherever and they ask to have a photo made with me. I'm not a celebrity and it doesn't happen every day. It's a cool thing when it does happen. Assuming I didn't smile like an idiot, I like to share those photos on my fan page. It puts the spotlight on them, and I can share who they are, how we met, and so on. It makes the community feel like a tight-knit group.

The key to a successful fan page is to have fun with it. Start conversations. Be a resource for people. And most importantly, focus on the fans. It's a privilege to have them.

36

Light the Fuse

WITHOUT A DOUBT the best way to promote your brand right now and for the rest of time is through word of mouth. There will never be a more powerful form of marketing. Word of mouth has been around since the beginning of time.

It's not what you say that counts. It's what others say about you that counts. People talk when they have something to talk about.

A happy customer is the best form of marketing. Don't just satisfy people. *Wow* them. Knock them off their feet (not literally, of course, or you'd be looking at a lawsuit). Your product and/or service shouldn't just be good. It should be excellent. You want customers to be thrilled they chose you. Regardless of what kind of business you are in, they experience business and that experience must be remarkable.

Customers need to come away energized and fired up. A great experience makes them eager to tell their friends. A mediocre or average experience ensures they don't tell a soul.

To create loyalty with your fans/audience, you must have a core message or promise that your fans can get behind. This core promise must *never* be broken under any circumstance.

You must be able to get your core message across in a few sentences. And you must be able to deliver on that promise consistently. If you can't, then you are in big trouble, my friend.

How passionate (and loyal) are your fans? If your business ended tomorrow, would anyone notice? You want your fans to be so passionate about you and your brand that it will live on long after you do.

Be remarkable and interesting. No one talks about boring companies or boring products. If you are boring, you are invisible. Don't create another piece of content, product, or ad unless it's worth talking about. People take notice when a company is different and does something worth talking about.

Most brands leave word of mouth up to chance. They fail to understand that you can ignite word of mouth. Although you can't control what people say, you can control what you do that makes them talk.

The more people like you and what you do, the more they will support your business. They get excited to tell their friends about you. Solve people's problems. Take care of them. Any trust you build up will be destroyed by not being good to people.

If people don't respect you, they won't talk about you. Not positively anyway.

If no one is talking about you, you need to start the conversation. Start spreading some positive word of mouth about your fans. It's important you acknowledge your fans and even support them in return. People love to be recognized and appreciated. Your fans are no different. You can strengthen the relationship with them by taking the spotlight off yourself and putting it on them.

If you want someone to be a fan of yours, start by being a fan of theirs. Treat your brand advocates like rock stars—because they are.

If you have employees, they should be your biggest fans. Smart businesses allow their employees to become brand advocates. Give your employees a voice. They're often the people who can best spread the word about your brand. If you are afraid of how they will use that voice, you need to reevaluate your hiring process.

> Make it easy for people to spread the word and share what you do.

If your fans have to go out of their way to spread the word, they won't. Even if they are your biggest fans, they won't. Make it easy on them by giving them the tools they need. Today's technology makes word of mouth happen at lightning speeds. Be prepared to take advantage of it.

All of your online content should be capable of being shared through social media networks with a single click. Pay attention to how easily YouTube has made it to share the videos. You can embed them directly on your website or post them on your social media profiles. You can e-mail your friends and family a direct link to the video. It's no wonder YouTube is such a success when it is so easy to share content.

Another way to ignite word of mouth is so simple but too few brands do it. Ask your fans to spread the word. Ask them for help. You're not too big to ask for help. Often people are more than happy to send you a referral or recommendation, but it's not going to be on the top of their mind. You have to give them that friendly little push.

Enthusiasm doesn't last. So you'll have to keep your fans excited. Look at how Apple rolls out new versions of their products. It keeps fans excited and keeps them talking. Heck, the very day the iPad came out, Apple fans were already debating what features the iPad 2 would have! Never let the dust settle on your fans.

Fans of your brand are more than just satisfied customers. Fans admire you, are inspired by you, and impressed with you. They like your personality and are impressed by your network and associations. They are in the best position to convince people to give you a shot. They are your most powerful ally.

Fans need to know they're appreciated for their efforts in helping you spread the word. Recognize them and show appreciation. Recognition means more than a gift.

37

Overnight Authority

ACTION IS THE KEY TO SUCCESS. One of the issues I have with most books is that they are full of theory and hype and lack actionable strategies that are proven to work. That's why I want to share with you the exact steps to implement a strategy I've used for years and hundreds of other entrepreneurs have used with great success. It's a strategy that will position you as a credible authority, increase your celebrity status, and give you lots of great content to share with your audience. Oh and the best part? It doesn't involve you spending money on ads or promotions.

I call it the interview authority method. Here's the gist of it. You interview a handful of experts and celebrities within your industry about their success and experience. Then you share those interviews on your website or blog for everyone to enjoy. Let's say you interview seven experts. That gives you several hours of great content your audience will enjoy. You can also have the audio interviews transcribed to give away as bonuses or use the interviews to entice people to subscribe to your e-mail list. The content the interviews give you are high quality and high value.

The power of association works here as well. When people listen to you interviewing these authorities, they begin to view you as an authority as well. It enhances your celebrity factor dramatically. It's no different than what Oprah did on her show or what Ryan Seacrest does on his radio show. Larry King did this for 25 years before he handed over the reins to Piers Morgan.

Interviewing people of authority in your industry also allows you to get on their radar. They get to know you a little bit, and you then have the chance to build a relationship with them. They become your ally, and many times they share their interview with their own audience thus creating more exposure for your brand and attracting new people to your site.

The one stumbling block people seem to run into when using this strategy is that they are afraid to ask someone for an interview. No one likes rejection, so I understand that. But it's actually a gazillion times easier than you think. Ninety-nine percent of the time you just have to ask. Others have a brand as well and they want exposure for it. Being interviewed by you is a great way for them to get their brand in front of new people who may not be familiar with them.

The first step in approaching them is to know how they prefer to be contacted. Typically, e-mail is the preferred choice, but you'll want to do your homework to be sure. Second, be flexible about their schedule. If you e-mail them on a Tuesday and want to interview them that Thursday, the answer is likely to be no. Fully explain to them what the interview will be about and explain why you want to interview them. It goes a long way when you can show them you know what they are about. Do your homework.

Another great little secret to getting someone to say yes to an interview is to ask them in person. It's easy to say no in an e-mail. It's much harder to do it face to face. It's not unusual for me to line up seven to ten interviews from attending one industry event.

As with asking someone for anything, it's always best if you have a relationship first. Get to know them through social media or something that is easy. Let the relationship grow and strengthen to the point where it's easy to ask because you already know the answer.

Another stumbling block people run into is what to ask these industry celebs. I like to get a little sneaky here, and I always ask them questions that I want to know the answers to. It's my way of getting some free advice. I always benefit from the knowledge I get from interviewing people. My focus is for my audience to learn something new, but if I learn something new in the process as well, that makes it extra awesome. Don't stress over questions. Have more questions prepared than you will need. I once interviewed someone who answered seven questions in less than 10 minutes. The interview was supposed to last for half an hour! I ran out of questions and ended up asking about what the person's favorite TV show was and how did he think *Lost* would end. Don't ask people tough questions. It's an interview, not an interrogation.

Don't assume that the only people worth interviewing are those who are well known in your industry. I personally love to listen to interviews from those undiscovered people who are making their business rock. I like to interview some of my clients from time to time, not only to help them gain some exposure but to showcase someone who isn't one of the usual suspects.

One of my favorite things about this strategy is that it works in any market. I've seen it work in industries such as fitness, karate, Internet marketing, health food, pets, finance, real estate, law of attraction, music, technology, leadership, faith, hypnosis, and skin care, just to name a few. I've interviewed some truly amazing entrepreneurs such as Seth Godin, Gary Vaynerchuk, Mark Joyner, and Yanik Silver. The first time I put this technique to use was in the real estate investing field. I wanted to educate real estate investors by giving them access to some of the rock stars in that world. I interviewed Than Merrill from the A&E TV show *Flip This House*. Than was a perfect person to interview because he was a celebrity in the real estate investing world with loads of credibility. Than also delivers phenomenal content and does it in a way that is easy to understand. That interview gave me additional exposure and credibility through the power of association.

This is a strategy that never gets old. Your blog readers will love this kind of content and will appreciate you for delivering it to them. As your brand grows, you will undoubtedly be asked to do an interview for someone. It's an honor to be asked. If your schedule allows it and it's a good fit, then do it. If not, let them down gently. And if you think my ramblings could be beneficial to your audience, then go to BrandAgainstTheMachine.com and drop me a line or hit me up on Twitter at twitter.com/johnmorgan. If I can fit it in my schedule and it's a good match, I'd be honored to do it. But don't hold it against me if I can't. ☺

38

Everything in Twos

HOW CONNECTED IS YOUR AUDIENCE with your brand? The goal is that they are very connected with you. The more connected they are with you, the more frequently they are exposed to your brand and the more they come to trust you.

The key is letting people connect with you on their terms. They have preferred channels they like to use that you may not. If you hate social media, but your audience loves it and hangs out there, then you'd better get your butt into social media.

Go where your prospects are. Use the networks and channels that they use. Hang out where they hang out.

Take Conan O'Brien, for example. After leaving *The Tonight Show*, or being forced out, Conan was without his platform. It would be several months before Conan would be on TV again and in front of his loyal fans. During this time Conan went to where his people were.

Conan created a Twitter account and began firing off one joke after another. He then launched a comedy tour allowing his audience to see him like never before. He stayed in front of his audience by connecting with them through multiple channels. He didn't wait to get back on the air to connect with his audience. He went to them.

You can't rely on just one method of connecting with people. Social media, e-mails, blogs, books, speeches, articles, and videos are all channels for connecting with people, just to name a few. You have plenty of options.

The worst number in business is the number one. You can't rely on one channel to connect with people. You can't rely on one method of generating leads and sales. The number one is dangerous. If that one method or channel is what your entire business is based on, you are playing with fire.

Google has caused a lot of stress for marketers who have built their entire business on Google's pay-per-click advertising channel. These marketers were making sales day and night virtually on autopilot. Then one day Google changed the rules and a lot of these marketers saw their sales stop immediately. They had to redo everything. Their business was fragile and was too reliant on one method.

You wouldn't build a table with just one leg, so don't build your business that way. Anyone who limits themselves to one channel or one anything is a fool. I recommend doing everything in twos as a minimum. So if you are going to use social media as a channel to connect, then use at least two networks like Facebook and Twitter, for example. If you send people a newsletter, also get connected with them via e-mail. Doing everything in twos is better than relying on one anything. But don't stop there.

There is not a "best way" to connect with people. That's another reason why you don't want to rely on a single method. The more ways someone is connected to you the faster and more likely he or she will become a client.

For example, I recently looked at the 10 people I interact with the most on Twitter. All 10 of them are also connected to me on Facebook. Seven are connected on LinkedIn, and several are getting my e-mail newsletter. Eight of those 10 I have since met face to face (after we met online) and 9 of those 10 are either clients, affiliates, or advocates for my business. Connecting through multiple channels is paying off.

The more connected you are with someone the better. But you have to give them a reason. If you don't give people a reason to connect with you, they won't.

One all-too-common problem with most brands is giving people a reason to connect with them on multiple channels. They use call to actions such as "check out my newsletter" and "Like us on Facebook."

Frankly, these call to actions suck. There is no reason *why* someone should connect with you there.

Why should they bother? What is in it for them?

People are always looking for their personal benefit. They never stop, and they never will. If you can clearly articulate that benefit and let them know exactly what's in it for them, you win.

If every piece of content on your e-mail newsletter, blog, and social media channels are the exact same, then there is no reason whatsoever for people to connect with you on more than one channel.

Where is the incentive to allow your brand into people's life through multiple channels? It has to be there or your efforts to connect will fall short.

Take your existing channels and break them down further. For example, it would make sense for people who read your blog to also get your e-mail newsletter. Give them a good reason to check out both. Social media is a great channel, but there are several social media sites you can use to connect with your audience. You need to be where your audience's eyes are.

You will certainly have one main channel that is your key platform. This is where you are most active and most comfortable. Let it be your foundation and allow your other channels to branch off from it.

My friend Perry Lawrence is an expert at using video to market businesses. It only makes sense that video is one of his best channels. However, Perry doesn't just rely on video alone. He uses e-mail marketing very effectively to connect with his audience and to bring them valuable content and information. Video is his comfort zone. It's his home base in terms of a platform. But it doesn't stop him from connecting via social media, public speaking, webinars, blogging, e-mail, and so on.

Is your brand only known through one channel? What would happen to your brand if Google, WordPress, or Facebook, for example, blew up? Technology and tools change all of the time. They are here today and gone tomorrow. Consistently connect with your audience on more than one channel. There is no such thing as being too connected to your target audience. Give them a real benefit for connecting with you everywhere.

39

Point of View

YOU KNOW THE SAYING that behind every great man is a great woman?
Well, behind every great brand is a great leader. Think of some of the
world's greatest brands such as Disney, Starbucks, Apple, Virgin, and
McDonald's. They all have had great leaders behind them such as Walt
Disney, Howard Shultz, Steve Jobs, Richard Branson, and Ray Kroc.

A great leader lets people know they are in good hands. They
display a passion that people will gravitate toward and follow. They
have a specific point of view on life or their industry that people can
rally behind. Every brand needs a great leader to be successful.

You are a leader if you realize it or not. It's time to start embracing
it. If you don't want to be a leader, then be aware that your audience
will find one to follow.

So what kind of leader does it take to run a successful business?
There are thousands of traits, but let's touch on a few key ones. Great
leaders have a positive, forward-thinking attitude. More than just seeing the positive in things, they find every reason to make something
work. *Quit* isn't in their vocabulary.

Great leaders are not afraid to challenge the status quo. How many
times has Richard Branson proved so-called experts wrong? More times
than he can count, I'm sure. Walt Disney made his life all about doing

the impossible. Steve Jobs's focus on innovation is something we should all learn from.

These great leaders aren't any different than you. You have the same amount of time in a day as they do. You don't have to flip your industry on its head to be considered a great leader. Even the smallest of brands can have a great leader behind them.

Leaders communicate big ideas. They get people on board with these big ideas. People are attracted to leaders as consumers and as employees. People are excited by ideas that they can rally behind.

Dave Ramsey is a leader. Dave helps people get out debt by giving them action steps along with a little bit of tough love. There is no shortage of people out there shelling out financial advice. So what makes Dave so popular and such a success? It's his leadership. Dave has ideas that are different than what a lot of financial experts teach. Dave's strategies for getting out of debt are to stop borrowing money and stop buying stuff you can't afford. It sounds simple, and it is. It's practical advice that people can get behind, especially because it works. Other financial teachers are so confusing it's hard to rally behind them. Dave's point of view is unique, refreshing, and one that is easy for others to buy into.

Of all of my friends and people I know, not one of them is a born leader. Okay, one of them is, but we don't like him very much. Leadership skills are something you learn and develop over time.

The biggest thing I see that great leaders have in common is their ability to focus and eliminate distractions. Distractions are killing entrepreneurs. Leaders keep pushing forward toward their goal. They don't slow down or succumb to distractions and interruptions.

Leaders have a vision and passion they communicate with others in a way that they become passionate about that vision as well. People rally behind those who lead them.

It doesn't matter if your business is large or small. It doesn't matter if your brand is only known in your local area or internationally. It's up to you to lead the way.

40

Back and Forth

THE MOST SUCCESSFUL BRANDS are the most consistent brands. You cannot expect someone to put his or her trust into you if there's a lot of back and forth in what you do. People do business with consistent people. They run away from businesses and people who are inconsistent.

Consistency isn't something that people find neat or nice. It's something they desperately want from a business. They aren't looking for a Johnny-come-lately or someone who's here-today-gone-tomorrow. They want to know they can depend on you. Consistency builds confidence with consumers. It shows you are a brand people can rely on. A brand that if they put their trust into, you won't let them down.

For someone to become a fan of yours or your business, you must let them know they can always count on you to deliver. You have to be consistent and reliable. Establish a brand pattern that your customers are familiar with. Doing business with you should be predictable. A customer should never be surprised unless it is a pleasant surprise.

Take McDonald's, for example. No matter which McDonald's you go to in the world, you know exactly what to expect. Sure, it's not the best food in the world, but that is beside the point. They have put the proper systems in place so that they can easily duplicate their service. It's no coincidence they are one of the largest brands in the world. If they were inconsistent from location to location, they wouldn't last.

Customers want to know that they can expect the same type of service and result if and when they choose to do business with you in the future. Your customers also want to know that if they tell their friends about you, you won't let them down. They don't want to look bad in front of their friends. Your consistency gives them confidence to spread the word about you.

For your target audience to remember you, you must be out there consistently. You must remain top of mind with your audience. You can't go in and out of the marketplace and expect people to be anxiously awaiting your return. It just doesn't work that way.

I'm often amazed at the amount of businesses that run a Super Bowl ad that one time during the game and then never run the ad again. Not only could the money for a Super Bowl commercial be better spent somewhere else, but the shelf life of the commercial and attention it receives is very short. One week later and you are out of people's minds—even sooner than a week in most cases. That is why consistency is so critical to your brand's success.

Every single area of your business has to be consistent. This means you need to deliver a quality product or service consistently that always delivers what is promised. Your customer service needs to be predictable and unwavering. The content you produce and your marketing has to be consistent. You must stay in front of people, or you risk losing customers to brands that are consistently more visible.

Let's take social media, for example, because it's an area where few people are consistent. Social media isn't a tool that can be used one month and then forgotten about until a few months later. You have to maintain a consistent presence there to be successful. Take a close look at the most successful brands in terms of social media. They are active virtually every day. The world moves too fast for an inconsistent brand to survive.

There must also be consistency throughout your brand and marketing. Your website shouldn't be one color scheme and your business cards another. Not that every element in your marketing has to match 100 percent, but it does have to have the same look and feel to it. You know an Apple product when you hold it. You don't need to see the Apple logo to know who made it. There is a familiarity to it. The branding is consistent and clear. Yours should be as well.

41

Feeling Good

AT SOME POINT IN TIME the fun must have been sucked out of most businesses. The overwhelming majority of businesses take themselves way too seriously. They also take their marketing efforts too seriously. They are causing their brand to be extremely boring.

This is actually a very serious problem. No one talks about things that are boring. When was the last time a friend said to you, "You have to see this movie, it's so incredibly boring!"? Exactly. The best way to ensure no one cares about your brand is to be boring.

A boring brand doesn't land on people's radar. You might as well not exist. Sometimes entrepreneurs are so concerned about coming across as professional that they forget we are all humans. Yes, being professional is great, but remember that you're doing business with people. There's a difference between being professional and being a boring stiff. People like to be entertained. Somewhere we lost the human element to our marketing and business. Unless you're reading this in the year 4025, you are a human. It's okay to act like it.

A little humor and a little silliness every now and again shows people you're approachable, and it adds a human element to your marketing. People respond well to humor, and they respond well to people that like to have fun.

Take YouTube.com's massive popularity, for example. It is full of silly dumb videos, and it's awesome (have you seen the one with the monkey riding backward on the back of a pig? Awesome). The point is that stupid stuff works. It appeals to everyone.

Deliver fun and entertaining messages. Let your hair down. You don't have to be a comedian for your customers to have a good time. You just have to stop being so serious all of the time. Zappos does a lot of things right as a brand. One of the best things they have done is create an amazing culture for their employees. It is a very fun environment to work in. Do they work hard? Yep. Do they have paper-wad fights in the middle of the day? Yep.

Employees don't dread going in to work at Zappos. Because they aren't sitting at their desk wishing they were dead, they are very productive. I've yet to come across anyone at Zappos who was in a bad mood. It's likely that I never will. Can you say the same about yourself and your employees?

Michael Bublé is an extremely talented singer. If you've seen one of his concerts, you know he's also a phenomenal performer. Amazingly, some of the most entertaining parts of his show are when there is no music at all. Michael takes time to interact and joke with the audience. He shares stories with them, asks them questions, and on many occasions jumps off the stage to go hug someone. For a guy who belts out love songs, it's not the quiet subdued show you would expect. Michael doesn't take himself too seriously, and it shows. He's having a good time, and the audience is having a good time with him. That is what it's all about. He's not concerned with being perfect. He's concerned with making sure everyone has fun. There's no doubt when people go to work the next day they are telling their friends about the show. He has built a great personal brand not only from his extraordinary talent, but also from his personality and charisma.

Richard Branson is another guy who certainly knows how to have a good time. There's an element of fun in every Virgin business. It starts with Richard and runs throughout the entire Virgin Company. Richard has plenty of serious things going on. His charity work alone would be a full- time job for most. But Richard also knows life is short, and if he's having fun and the people he works with are having fun, then so will the customer. Many of Richard's crazy stunts certainly generate a great amount of press, but more than that they show the fun side of the Virgin brand.

You may be in a very serious industry, but that is no excuse for your business to be boring. Don't take yourself too seriously, and don't take what you do too seriously. Your business should be fun for you, your employees, and for your customers. People gravitate toward fun people and businesses. You have my permission to let your hair down.

42

Everything You Do Is Branding

SOMEONE IS WATCHING YOU. Sounds kind of creepy, doesn't it? Your brand is always on display. People are always paying attention, so be aware. *Transparency* is a word that is tossed around far too often in my opinion. What does it even mean to be transparent? Most mean it as being real: being open with your audience, and proving you have nothing to hide.

That's all well and good, but the reality is that you are transparent whether you like it or not. It's not a strategy like some so-called gurus will tell you. You don't implement transparency. You're always being transparent because you're always being watched.

> Everything you do is branding.

Every conversation you have is branding.

Every person you associate with is branding.

Everything you wear is branding.

Everything you say is branding.

Everywhere you hang out is branding.

Everything you don't do is branding.

143

You are constantly being evaluated and judged. Your personal brand encompasses everything about you: who you associate with, how you dress, your sense of humor, your hobbies, your style, your charisma, and your abilities. So you must be aware that your brand is in the spotlight 24/7.

> Your brand either works for you or against you, but it always works.

A friend of mine has a bad habit of constantly complaining about her job. It's what she talks about 90 percent of the time. Of course, everything bad about her job is the boss's fault. She's the perfect employee. This negativity and bad mouthing of her boss made me realize I would never recommend that someone hire her. She was looking for a new job and asked if I knew anyone. The answer was no, whether I knew someone or not. The conversations you have are branding.

> Your brand is always on.

Michael Phelps is one of the most amazing Olympians of all time. Watching him destroy record after record in the 2008 Beijing Olympics was something I will never forget. Something that Michael will never forget is that people are always watching. In 2009 photos were taken of Michael at a party that showed him using a bong, which is a device used for smoking marijuana for those of you who don't know. I had to look it up myself. The press had a field day tearing down one of the greatest athletes of all time. Michael will never forget that his brand is always on display.

You're not just being watched in the real world. Online you are being watched by thousands. Everything you do online is seen. This means that Facebook picture of you dominating a game of beer pong may not be the best image for your brand.

> You are in public when you are online. Act accordingly.

Be open and approachable. You can't hide from your customers nor should you. Most old school corporate-type brands are scared to death of transparency. Trying to hide is a big mistake. You can't hide forever. Trying to be someone you're not is a big mistake. You can't keep it up forever.

Your brand and your business are in the wide open. Everything you do has an effect on your brand. Transparency is not a choice; it is a must.

43

Hidden Brand Advocates

AS AN EMPLOYEE AT ONE OF DISNEY'S THEME PARKS, you cannot do any of the following while "on stage": smoke, eat, drink, sit down, chew gum, sleep, fold your arms, or lean against a railing or wall. Seems a bit much, but it's not. Disney understands better than most that every employee is an extension of your brand.

Disney wants the experience their customers have to be one they will remember the rest of their lives. They know that nothing can kill the mood at the "Happiest Place on Earth" quicker than a bad experience with an employee.

Each and every employee on payroll represents your brand. As brand ambassadors, they are your soldiers on the ground. The interaction they have with customers greatly influences how people feel about your brand.

Just the other day I drove past a grocery store that had a big sign right outside the front door promoting healthy food choices. It would have been nice except that a mere five feet away was the store manager on his break, smoking. I'm not a smoker, and I certainly don't want to smell smoke right before I walk into a grocery store to select my healthy food choices. The manager was on his break, so it shouldn't count right? Wrong.

In terms of branding, it *always* counts.

Have you ever called a doctor's office to schedule an appointment and found a very rude secretary on the other end of the line? I know I sure have, and I'm guessing you have as well. It's doubtful that the doctor is even aware that the person on her front line is hurting her brand.

Not to beat up on doctors specifically, but last year I went to the doctor for a pain in my chest that ended up being a broken sternum. How I broke the sternum is another story I'll save for the sequel. While sitting in the waiting room with a few other sickies, I heard the two ladies behind the front desk complaining just about everything. They were complaining about the cars they drive, their husbands being lazy, and had some harsh things to say about a coworker who called in sick that day. I went in for a chest pain, but by the time I saw the doc I wanted some antidepressants!

Every element of your business supports your brand or tears it apart. Employees are no exception to that. They represent your brand on and off the clock.

Your company culture can greatly dictate what kind of interaction your customers will have with your employees. Simply put, if they are happy and excited to be at work, the customers will know. If they have clocked in but wish they were dead, then your customers will know.

Creating a great culture and atmosphere for your employees isn't something that can be done with a flip of a switch. You have to be the example. You set the tone for the rest of the company.

In consulting with some of the largest brands in the world, I've seen an interesting commonality among the most successful of them. They educate and train their employees like their brand depends on it. And it does. At no point should you stop training your employees. Help them improve and grow. Give them the space and encouragement to get better. They will be happier because of it, and they will go the extra mile for your business. This causes a trickle effect all the way down to your customers.

An employee who isn't in line with what your brand is about is not worth keeping around. Spend more time on the hiring process and more time training those who make the cut. Great employees can leave a customer with a great feeling about your brand. Reward them for their efforts and behavior. They are an important tool in your arsenal.

44

Come as You Are

WE ARE NOT SUPPOSED TO JUDGE PEOPLE based on appearances alone. Yet we do. Every one of us makes assumptions and forms opinions about people based on their image. We judge more than people. We judge buildings, packaging, and vehicles.

If you went to the doctor and the parking lot was all broken up with huge cracks and holes in it, you wouldn't be too impressed. If inside the office you found a lovely 1970s decor and plastic plants, you would start to get a little nervous. You'd begin to question how up to speed this doctor really is.

If you went to the grocery store and saw a colorful box of well-packaged cookies sitting next to a generic box that simply said "cookies," you're going to assume the one with better packaging tastes better. You're not judging based on taste, you're judging based on appearance.

We all judge things based on appearance. Every element of your business affects your brand's image. Imagine for a second that you are listening to someone speak about fitness. You find their tips on eating healthy and exercising to be very helpful. So you go to their website to possibly purchase one of their courses or products, and you find a website full of clip art that looks like an eight-year-old made it. You aren't going to be too impressed.

148

I'm not a big fan of business cards. For the most part I find that they are irrelevant, but my biggest issue with them is that 99.9 percent of them are boring. Of course, if you attend any type of networking event you're going to have people throwing business cards at you like candy. There's an idea, a business card made of candy. I would love that. Anyway, I met a guy once who was a nice enough dude. He asked me for a business card, and when I told him I didn't have one he looked at me with great horror in his eyes.

Once he realized the world didn't end, he proceeded to give me his business card even though I didn't ask for it. He told me he sold some service that would skyrocket sales and blah blah blah. I don't remember because I wasn't really listening. Whatever he sold it wasn't cheap, as he made sure to let me know three different times.

When he walked away I looked at my hand and realized there was black ink on my fingers. My first thought was that he gave me some sort of disease, but that was just my OCD talking. Turns out it was ink rubbing off his cheap business card. His card had perforated edges where he must have printed them on huge sheets from Office Max. Wait, it gets better. The back of his card read: "Call 1-800-555-0000 for Your FREE Box of 100 Business Cards!"

His business card did not make me want to do business with him. It wasn't at all congruent with the price he charges or the service he provides. His brand image is wrong on so many levels.

> Your image has to be congruent with your brand.

There are a lot of people who like to get a caricature or cartoon of themselves made and use that as their photo online and on print materials. This is a no-no. Look, I get it, and there was a time in my life when I was going to be a cartoonist. The problem is that you are not a cartoon in real life. It has to be the real you.

Another element of your brand image is the color scheme you use. I could get real geeky on you right now and go into great detail about the feelings each color on the color wheel convey, but I won't. I won't do that because ultimately any colors work. There's not a right or wrong color. You just need to pick one theme and run with it. Keep it consistent on everything you do. Don't waste time stressing over what colors to go with. My best advice is to pick a color scheme you won't get sick of down the road.

The colors with my brand are pretty much always red, white, and black. I'm often asked why that is. The answer has nothing to do with emotion or some psychological effect on the mind. It's because I like those colors, I happen almost always to wear black, and it's my own tiny tribute to The White Stripes, who are one of my favorite bands of all time.

Pick colors that work for you and own them. Make them your own. Don't think it to death. They are colors; they are supposed to be fun.

Logos are another area people get bent out of shape about. I love a good logo. I view logos as art. That said, let me drop a bomb on all you logo designers out there: no one buys something because the logo looks good. Like colors, don't overthink your logo. What matters is consistency and using your logo on everything you do. That's how a logo works regardless of how awesome it is or is not.

The main thing to keep in mind with your logo is that simple is best. Think of the best logos in the world. Most of them are simple, one or two colors, and they are very basic when it comes right down to it. Google, Virgin, Shell, LG, Sony, FedEx, and Nike's logos all have something in common. They are simple and clean. That's what makes a good logo.

You can certainly have a logo designed that supposedly invokes some subliminal meaning. But those are costly. Your money is better spent elsewhere. A lot of great designers online can get you a great logo. 99Designs.com is a great place to get a logo because you can control your budget. They have designers from all over the world giving you design options.

The packaging of your products is a great branding tool. Your materials should look good. You don't want a website that looks like it was built in 1999. Packaging has a great effect on your brand. Packaging is part of the experience for your customers. Apple's products come in brilliant packaging. How good is their packaging? People are selling the empty boxes their iMac came in on eBay. That's how good it is. Awesome and unique packaging can make your brand stand out and get people talking about it.

How you dress and look matters. I know that stinks, but it's true. Your appearance has to match your audience and brand. If your audience is attorneys, they probably won't be too impressed with you wearing shorts and sandals. That is unless that's exactly what your brand is about. Congruency must be present.

We all know the importance of knowing our target audience. Knowing them helps us create value and give them what they want and what they need. But have you ever stopped to see if your brand fits your customers?

If your brand doesn't fit them, then it's an uphill battle for sales. Your brand has to resonate with them. There has to be some congruency between you and them.

Let me give you an example. If you sell products in the model train niche (wish I could come up with a less boring example) but in all of your videos, photos, and so on, you portray your image as a surfer dude, then your audience is going to find it very difficult to relate and bond with you. If your audience can't relate to you, then your brand is as good as dead.

Use the same language as they do. There's a certain terminology that is common to an industry that may seem foreign to outsiders. Speaking the same language as your audience shows that you know them. It shows that you are one of them.

Your lifestyle plays more of an important role than you know. If your audience is predominantly single, they may not resonate with you talking about taking your kids to the park and changing diapers. But if your audience does have children, then they will feel a connection with you. In their eyes you are just like them.

All of this comes down to having a consistent image with your message and with your audience. Each element of your brand is either helping you or hurting you. Create an image that is authentic and genuine for you. Keep it consistent and congruent, and you'll have an image that works.

45

The 20/60/20 Rule

THE MORE YOU GROW YOUR BRAND and the more your presence and awareness increases, you will find that people will generally fall into one of three categories. I call it the 20/60/20 rule, and if leveraged properly you'll create a massive community of raving fans.

Twenty percent of people will love you and everything you do. No matter what. Unless you do something really horrible (like Tiger Woods).

Sixty percent will be on the fence. They either aren't familiar with you or they haven't made up their mind about you yet. They can take you or leave you.

Twenty percent will hate you. No matter what. These people don't match your personality and weren't hugged enough as a child. They thrive on hating what is popular. Don't worry about these people because they were never going to buy from you anyway. And in fact, their hate toward you is actually a good thing because it lights a fire in your fans.

As you become a more visible brand, you will find you are constantly being watched. Some people will respect and admire you. Some people will be jealous of you, and some people will flat out hate you. Sounds fun, doesn't it? It's not such a bad thing.

Haters drive your raving fans who love you crazy. It unites your fan base. They'll fight for you and defend you. Don't believe me? Go to a group of teenage girls and tell them the Twilight series sucks. Or try telling someone who owns an iPod, iPhone, and iPad that Apple isn't the best in the business. Look at the passion and fire in their eyes as they defend what they love.

Your supporters will stick up for you and they will fight for you. It strengthens the bond between you and your audience who loves you.

> The number one thing you don't want is for people to be indifferent about your brand.

We see this all of the time with politicians. Maybe you are for the president or maybe you are against the president. Either way, when someone attacks "your guy," you want to fight back.

My good friend Darren Crawford once wrote something slightly negative on Twitter about the band Collective Soul. In no time he was receiving replies from Collective Soul fans telling him he's crazy. Even the band responded from their Twitter account! The 20 percent that love the band came to their defense, and quickly my friend was outnumbered.

It is human nature to want to be liked, but understand you are never going to please everyone. Having haters is unavoidable. No brand can have universal appeal. You have to develop a thick skin about it, and you have to focus on those who love you.

Not everyone will be a fan of yours. And that's okay because you don't want everyone. You want the *right* people. There are enough people in the world not to have to work with the douchebags. This is why the 60 percent on the fence are dangerous. You don't want them on the fence. You want to know exactly where they stand one way or the other. The quicker you get them to make up their mind, the better.

You also have to know the difference between someone hating you and someone giving you honest feedback. There is a difference between someone being a critic and someone being a jerk.

Real feedback is not full of insults and hate. Actual criticism is genuine. It's that person's opinion and they are entitled to it. Be thankful they are voicing it so that you know what areas you need to improve. It's the people who never say a word who should greatly concern you. They aren't into you, and you have no idea why.

Being 100 percent honest with you, it doesn't feel good when someone doesn't like you or your business. My first response when someone critiques me is never overwhelming joy and appreciation for their honesty. My first reaction is to tell them they are stupid and ugly and that no one loves them. Even though honest feedback can be very hurtful, it is something you must accept. Real feedback from your audience and customers should be taken very seriously. Constructive criticism is something you must be open to. Don't run from it—embrace it.

Haters, in contrast, aren't worth the energy. Don't waste time trying to win them over because you won't. Focus your energy on taking excellent care of your supporters and fans.

> When your brand stands for something, you are guaranteed to have haters.

Marketing legend Dan Kennedy says if you aren't pissing off at least one person a day, you aren't trying hard enough. Don't let a few negative people stop you from sharing your message and helping others. Focus on those who appreciate and value what you do.

In fact, screw the haters. Put everything you've got toward the 20 percent of people who get value out of what you do. The 20 percent of people who need your help are the people highly interested in you, and those are the people spending money. The other 20 percent aren't making you a dime.

Don't fuel people's hate with a response. Again, respond to a genuine critic or customer complaint, but let the haters hate. After all, life is short. Why waste your time with scum?

Regardless of what someone says about your brand, you can chime in on your side of the story and let everyone come to their own decision.

Haters are the reason brands often freak out about social media because they feel they don't have control of their message. News flash: You never had control. People have always been talking about you;

it's just that prior to social media you had to be standing right next to them to hear it.

Negative people aren't worth your attention. They will throw you off your game and bring you down. Take comfort in knowing that the haters were never going to become clients anyway. You have fans and supporters. Give them everything you have got. Let the haters hate.

46

The Real Thing

WHAT DOES IT MEAN TO BE AN AUTHENTIC BRAND? *Authenticity* is a word tossed around a lot in marketing circles. Being authentic simply means that you are who you say you are. Being authentic inspires trust. The more transparent and authentic you are, the more likely people will believe what you have to say.

People who are authentic do what they say they are going to do. If you make a promise or marketing claim and can't follow through on it, then the level of trust you've established with people takes a big hit. Authenticity with your marketing and your actions is critical to building trust with people.

Prospects are constantly trying to weed out legitimate experts from self-proclaimed gurus. You are constantly being evaluated as to whether you deserve someone's trust. People are searching for elements that prove your authenticity and validate you. The easier it is for people to see you have nothing to hide, the better. The best way for people to see you are authentic is by your actions. How you behave reveals more about your authenticity than anything you could ever say.

When a brand is congruent with what they say and what they do, people trust them. It sounds simple because it is. Yet for some reason people tend to struggle with this. Authenticity counts in everything you do. Honesty and transparency never lose their importance.

Don't pretend to be someone you are not. Be real and allow people to see the good, the bad, and the ugly. Sadly, most brands are afraid to peel back the curtain and give you a behind-the-scenes look. Keller Williams Realty is one of the largest real estate companies in the world. They have an open-book policy with their agents. Any Keller Williams Realty agent can see the health of the company at any time. Other real estate companies never open their books to their agents. Does this mean they have something to hide? Not necessarily. It does mean that they are not as transparent as their competition and have to work harder to establish trust.

The Internet has created a whole new need for brands to be authentic and transparent. It's far too easy for someone to hide behind their keyboard. Consumers doing business online want to know who they are dealing with. There are several ways to ease any concerns that prospects may have about your authenticity.

Use real photos in all of your marketing materials. This is especially the case in social media. I don't want to be Facebook friends with a logo. People want to connect with people. A nice head shot of you is a must. And by "nice head shot" I don't mean a Glamour Shots photo of you from 10 years ago. And I certainly don't mean a photo of you holding a stack of money. People holding a wad of cash in their profile photo deserve to be punched in the kidneys.

Maintaining a consistent social media presence is an excellent way to display your authenticity. Your target audience can connect with you on multiple channels, and they can see how you engage with others. Allowing people to engage with you lets them get to know you. They get a feel for your personality and can begin to make a safe assumption on whether or not you deserve their trust.

Showcasing your testimonials whenever possible provides a tremendous amount of proof and authenticity. Testimonials back up your claims and let prospects know you follow through on your promises.

Finally, sometimes the best way to establish yourself as an authentic brand is to respond to people in a timely fashion. How long does it take you to return phone calls and respond to e-mails? Professionals get back to people quickly. If someone has a hard time getting in touch with you, they will give up.

It is understandable that you want to put your best foot forward. Yet some people confuse putting their best foot forward with putting up a fake persona. Being fake is a sure way to destroy any loyalty people have with your brand. You simply can't keep it up. It will catch up with you. Misleading your fans is never a good idea. Give people more credit. They value honesty and openness.

Robert Downey Jr. is a superb actor who certainly has his share of flaws. His past struggles with drug use have been well documented. Robert is extremely authentic with his personal brand and openly discusses his past troubles. He never hides it and will often poke fun of himself regarding his troubles with addiction. This makes his fans very comfortable. They know exactly what they are getting with him. Is he perfect? Far from it. But he has never tried to be something he is not.

Tiger Woods, in contrast, has become an excellent example of the importance of having an authentic brand. He was once one of the largest and best personal brands in the world. Beyond his enormous golf talent, Tiger was branded as a quiet, simple family guy. We all know now that persona wasn't completely accurate. When it was revealed that Tiger had a history of infidelity, a lot of his fans felt betrayed. It's not that his personal life is anyone's business. It's that he was sold to his fans as being someone he wasn't.

Take a look back at Tiger's brand before it came off the tracks, and you will realize his fans actually knew very little about him. He was quiet and guarded. We only knew the Tiger we saw on the golf course. Tiger was keeping some big secrets from the public and from his fans, secrets that were impossible to keep forever. Sooner or later the truth comes out.

Being authentic means you have nothing to hide. You have strengths and weaknesses, and all of them are visible. No one is perfect, and your fans don't expect you to be. What they do expect is for you to be transparent and genuine with them. Actually, they don't expect it—they demand it.

47

What's in a Name?

IS THERE SUCH A THING AS THE PERFECT BRAND NAME? Nope. The perfect brand name doesn't exist. Sure, there are good brand names and there are bad brand names. Actually some are really bad. But the truth is that any name can be made to work.

Imagine for a second that a friend was launching a new business and wanted your opinion on the name. What would your response be if the person said Google or Virgin or Zappos? Most likely you wouldn't be blown away. Yet all of those brand names work extremely well. But they work because of what they do, not because of the name.

People don't do business with you because of your name or the name of your product or business. They do business with you because of what you do and the solution you provide to their problem.

> A good brand name should be distinctive and memorable. It should be easy to pronounce and easy to read.

In terms of your personal brand, people sometimes struggle with branding their own name or the business name. You have to brand both. As your business grows, your personal brand will grow as well.

159

They are one and the same. When Apple or Virgin has success, it only enhances the personal brands of Steve Jobs and Richard Branson.

Because everyone in the world is online these days, getting your name to stand out is a challenge. When I was born my parents decided to give me the most popular name in existence. In fact, I graduated high school with two other John Morgans. One of them even had the same middle name as me!

Because my name is ridiculously common, showing up in search engine results can be a challenge. I've debated going by my full name, John Michael Morgan, or even coming up with a nickname to go by. However, everyone knows me as John Morgan. To start going by any other name would seem silly.

So does poor search engine optimization hurt my business? Nope. I'm not saying it's not important, but there are so many other ways to build your brand and increase exposure. And although there are over 32 million results that come up when you Google my name, I'm not afraid of the challenge. I focus on putting out great content and building my brand so that although I'm not the only John Morgan, I'm certainly one of the best.

Celebrities change their names all of the time to something that they think sounds cooler. I suppose Tom Cruise does sound better than Thomas Cruise Mapother IV. But there's nothing wrong with just going by the good old name your parents gave you. Comedian Zach Galifianakis has a last name that is kind of hard to pronounce. He could have changed it, but instead he decided to own it. After all, it is his name.

Although names are important, don't waste time dwelling on it. You can easily overthink it. And I can assure you that you're putting more thought into it than your audience will.

48

The Prospect Cycle

MOST BUSINESSES KEEP SHOVING ADS IN OUR FACE until we go insane. They continue to interrupt us hoping that eventually they will wear us down and we'll give in. They don't care that we aren't waiting in anticipation to see their ad. For example, no one looks forward to a TV commercial unless they have to pee. Interruption is not the way to move someone from being a prospect to becoming a customer.

> Results do not come from marketing that is based on intrusion.

Somewhere along the way we forgot that it's real people buying our products and services. Stop focusing on marketing so much, and start focusing on people. When you focus on people, your brand will quickly reflect that.

You see, the old way of promoting a brand was to go around *telling* the world about it. It wasn't very effective. Then brands started getting a little smarter and began *showing* people what they do rather than telling them. The results weren't much better. The future of marketing is based on *involving* people. This will create massive results. The interest level increases with each method.

Your prospect cycle should look something like this:

Strangers turn into prospects.

Prospects turn into fans.

Fans turn into customers.

Customers turn into advocates.

Your marketing funnel should be based on moving someone through this cycle and building a relationship with them along the way. Each step should be geared toward earning their trust and establishing your credibility.

> The brand with the most trust wins.

Is there room for your brand in today's overcrowded marketplace? The answer is yes, *if* you make room. Make people stand up and take notice. When they notice you and begin to look into what you are all about, they go from a stranger to a prospect. The cycle at this point has begun.

Understand that the better prospects can get to know you, the quicker they will become a fan. If they can't get to know you, then they may never like you. Your ability to create rapport with people is a major factor in your brand's success. People love to see a commonality they have with you.

Your focus should always be on moving people through your prospect cycle. This is why you should never stop campaigning for your brand. An effective branding campaign moves people from prospect to customer and then hopefully into loyal advocates of your brand.

Credibility is a key ingredient in your brand. The more people come in contact with your brand, the more chances you have to showcase your credibility. The more credibility you have, the easier it is to promote your brand.

> Intentions do not equal dollars.

As your prospects move through the cycle, they will watch what you do. What you say becomes far less important. Many brands have failed despite having the best of intentions. Once a company representative told me their mission statement positioned them as an authority. I nearly threw up in my mouth. Your mission statement is garbage. Can you recall a single mission statement from any company you've done business with? Of course you can't. Because mission statements don't mean a thing to customers.

> What you do makes your brand a success, not what you say.

Don't create a marketing funnel based on the old rules of marketing. You'll fall into the same trap as every other business. Marketing must be based on relationships and not impressions. That is what works and what will continue to work in the future. Conventional marketing leads to conventional results.

49

Viva La Failure

WARNING: YOU ARE GOING TO screw up. No need to get upset; just accept it and move on. No person in this world is perfect, and there is certainly no such thing as a perfect brand. Everyone makes mistakes. It has happened to you before, and it is going to happen to you again.

Don't think for a second that you will make all of the right decisions. You will hire someone you shouldn't. You will say something you will regret immediately after the last word leaves your lips. You will implement a new idea and it will fail. You will launch a new product that won't sell.

I'm not going to spend a lot of time telling you to pick yourself back up after you fail. You know that already. But I do want you to know that the brand that never tries something new is the brand that will be passed by those willing to be innovative. Those who are willing to fail will win. Don't fear failure. Embrace it.

The challenge is not letting the fear of failure stop you. You won't always do the right thing, and people will see you mess up. Today your mistakes are visible to everyone. This is a frightening thought for most people. You have to understand that it's okay to screw up as long as you make it right. People are forgiving by nature.

If you handle your disaster the right way, you will be okay. The reality is that people forget over time, and they can forgive. Remember as a kid when you were taught that honesty is the best policy? Guess what? It still is. Be up front and honest with your audience and customers when you make a mistake. They just want to see what you are doing to correct it.

Complaints about your brand used to be handled in private. Today they are online and open for the world to see. They also hang around in cyberspace forever. No brand has a clean record. It's okay for these mistakes to be public. Monitoring your blog comments or deleting negative comments on your Facebook fan page are a bad idea. You cannot hide.

A local coffee shop in my town has made the attempt to run and hide from their mistakes. When a customer had a complaint, he voiced it with the owner. When the issue wasn't resolved, the customer turned to Twitter. This is where things got messy. The coffee shop responded via Twitter and started an argument with the customer. It wasn't pretty. Coming across as defensive is not a good brand strategy.

The coffee shop ended up deleting their Twitter account and then started over with a new one. Rather than acknowledging the customer's issue and working with the person toward a solution, they attacked the customer then ran and hid. You can't just delete your mistakes and pretend they never happened.

Acknowledgment of a mistake goes a long way with people. More than an apology, people want to know how you are correcting the problem. BP's legendary oil spill in the Gulf Coast caused many people to want to burn the company to the ground. Most people were less concerned about destroying BP and more concerned about how they were going to fix the problem. They were looking for BP to give them a plan of how they were going to handle it. Don't leave people in the dark. Admit your mistake; make things right, and keep moving forward.

> A brand can be destroyed in an instant.

Brands make mistakes on social media channels all of the time. Some of these mistakes are small, and some are quite large. When a brand posts something it shouldn't on Twitter, all of their followers immediately begin looking for the same thing. The next tweet should acknowledge they messed up. How you handle a crisis is critical. The worst way to handle it is to pretend it didn't happen.

If you screw up but don't own up to it, you're going to make things worse. You have to know how to handle a crisis. The best way to do that is to acknowledge the error and bend over backward to make it right.

Not every failure has to do with offending someone or causing oil spills. Coca-Cola made one of the largest mistakes in business history when they introduced "new Coke." Their customers hated it, and Coke took a hit. But Coke listened to their audience and went back to the version people knew and loved. They admitted it was a mistake. They are still one of the largest brands in the world. Although the idea they took action on didn't work out in this case, at least they tried something, and that should always be respected.

Mistakes are progress as long as you keep moving.

Great brands execute. They aren't afraid of trying new things. They aren't afraid of failing. Great brands never stop when they fail. They focus on solutions and not problems.

Understand that anytime you do something out of the ordinary, you are going to face self-doubt. There is a certain level of fear that comes with every risk. You cannot afford to let fear of failure stop you from executing. Execution is far more important than ideas. A million-dollar idea isn't worth a thing unless you take action on it.

Energy and enthusiasm are only effective if they lead to action. Too many people are afraid to try something new until they think it's perfect. They don't want to make a mistake publicly. You don't have to live with a decision forever. Make a decision, and if it doesn't work, adjust and adapt. Fix it along the way. It's okay to fail. Stop overplanning and worrying about details.

Get out there and make stuff happen. Don't let the fear of messing up keep you from taking action and implementing new ideas. The worst thing that can happen is that you will have made a horrible mistake.

Don't sit around telling the world what you intend to do. Show the world. Failing is a better result than doing nothing at all.

Many people are competitive by nature. Therefore their business is competitive. They don't just want to beat the competition; they want to destroy the competition. I don't think there is anything wrong with that. After all, if you're not trying to be the best, then why are you trying at all?

50

Know Your Enemy

BE CAREFUL OF PUTTING too much focus and attention on a competitor. You don't want to fall into the trap of obsessing and worrying about what your competition is doing. Focus on your business, and let them worry about themselves.

Too often businesses make the mistake of examining what everyone in their industry does. This is a mistake because your business will end up looking like everyone else's. If you want ideas and inspiration for your business, look at industries outside of your own. Stop following the same approach as everyone else!

My friend and mentor Craig Proctor did that with his real estate business. Craig noticed that virtually every car dealer offered a trade-up program. You know how it works. Come in to buy one of their cars and they buy yours. It's been done for ages. Craig took what was very common for one industry and brought it into his. He implemented a trade-up program for homebuyers. If you move up and buy one of his listings, he'll buy your existing home. This value proposition was a huge boost for his brand and business. The real estate industry had never seen anything like it.

Craig's competition hated it, obviously. They were too focused on how everyone else was doing it to look outside their industry for innovative ideas. Craig has been one of the top RE/MAX agents in the world for what seems like forever. He's achieved that by thinking outside of the box and doing what his competition is afraid to do.

Competition is not a bad thing. A little competition is healthy for your business. Bigger brands and tough competition force you to be better and force you to raise your game. They push you to the next level.

It always saddens me when I see someone hate their competition. Yes, you want to win. You want to be better than your competitors. But don't be obsessed with always winning. The other guy can win some as well. Competition is good for customers. The more people competing for their business, the better products and services they get.

Don't attempt to build up your brand by tearing down others because it won't work. Every time you try to bring someone down, you end up looking just as bad. Sometimes you end up looking worse.

Promoting yourself by trashing your competition is a form of jackassery that won't be accepted. There is no need for it, and it makes you seem very uncreative.

You have to keep an open mind about your competition. Oftentimes they have the potential to be a great ally of yours. You never know when a competitor will turn into a partner. I've partnered with three competitors before on various projects. We understand there is enough business out there for everyone. If we can help each other out and help our audience, then great. I'm proud to say I'm a close friend with several of my competitors as well and not in a keep-your-enemies-close kind of way. I'm truly happy to see them succeed, as long as they don't succeed more than me.

Is your competition really competition?

I met Paul Evans while speaking at an event in Houston, Texas. Paul teaches entrepreneurs how to create information products they can then sell online. His audience and my audience are often similar. We often speak at the same events, and a good portion of our audience is familiar with both of us. Does that make us competitors? Yes and no.

Although we are often marketing to the same people, Paul and I do different things. We help the same people but we do help them in two different ways. Had Paul and I viewed each other as competitors, we both would have missed a great opportunity to help each other. I support Paul's business, and he supports mine. Paul is not only a business ally of mine, but he's a great friend, a friend I wouldn't have gotten to know had I simply viewed him as the competition.

This doesn't mean you have to become best buddies with your competition. It is often motivating to have an enemy. Just don't focus all of your energy on them. Every ounce of energy you waste worrying about what your competition is up to, is energy you should be spending on your customers.

Be aware of what your competitors do, but don't obsess about it. Implementing something in your business because a competitor does it is ludicrous. This happens all of the time. One business starts something new, and next thing you know, everyone in their industry is doing it that way. You have no idea if what you are copying is even working for them.

While looking through a publication I came across a competitor of mine that was word for word ripping off two of my ads. Basically, they just took my name off and slapped their name on. I was in shock. Not because I was copied. I was shocked because the two ads I ran in that publication were a complete flop. They didn't generate a single lead.

I knew the ads didn't work, but my competition did not. They blindly copied something just because a competitor of theirs was doing it. They assumed the ads worked. I'm sure they ended up scratching their heads wondering where they went wrong. Of course, I never told them.

In that case the competition was foolish, but that is not always true. Don't underestimate your competition. They are a lot smarter than you think—except for the dumb ones.

51

Erase, Then Replace

IT IS TIME TO ADDRESS SOMETHING few businesses do, yet alone talk about. I am about to tell you why you should never hesitate to fire a client. The idea of firing a client leaves many in shock. I suppose that's because it seems to go against what we are trying to accomplish in business. It's a hard paradigm shift for some because they never want to turn away the chance to make money.

Bad clients will cost you. They will do far more harm than good, regardless of how much money you stand to make from them. Trust me when I say that some clients are just not worth the effort.

Whoever said "the customer is always right" is an idiot. That would only be true if all customers were perfect. Your customers are human, and no one is perfect. Not all customers are created equal. We need a new phrase that says "sometimes the customer is a douchebag."

Early in my real estate career, I had a horrible client. Let's call him Satan. I received a phone call from Satan asking me to come out to his home and talk with him about putting it up for sale. During my sales presentation, Satan was a little rude but nothing worth me getting terribly upset about. I listed his home and crossed my fingers for a fast sale. As luck would have it, the very next day after his home went on the market, we received a full-price offer! I felt like a hero and quickly thought I must be the greatest agent of all time.

His response to the full-price offer after only being on the market 24 hours stunned me. He rejected the offer. No counteroffer or negotiation. He just rejected it. His reasoning was that if a full price offer came that quickly, then maybe he would get an offer greater than his asking price a few weeks later.

Naturally, I was quite frustrated. After that, the home sat on the market for another five months before we finally received a second offer. Luckily he accepted it with no problem.

After managing the transaction and dealing with his negative and condescending attitude for weeks, we finally went to close escrow. That's when things went from bad to worse. After reviewing the closing documents, I noticed a way I could save my client $2,000. The attorney went to work on the changes I suggested, which delayed our closing by an hour. Now, you would think a normal person who just saved $2,000 would be okay with closing a little late. But not Satan. He was pissed.

He yelled at me, telling me I was a moron and slammed his hands on the table. Rather than being appreciative for the savings I found him, he was mad about closing late.

During my time working with Satan, I put up with a lot of crap. He was rude to everyone I saw him come in contact with. He wasn't worth putting up with. He took up so much energy that it exhausted me. He took time away from clients I enjoyed working with.

Today, I have a policy in my business called the "No Jackasses Allowed" policy. Very professional sounding, don't you think? The reason this policy has been put into place is because one jerk of a client will cost you time, energy, and money. They will throw you off of your game. I suggest you implement a similar policy in your business as well, even if you are just starting out.

You don't want to spend your focus dealing with them because they will take time away from your cool clients who appreciate what you do. If a client doesn't match your profile of what an ideal client looks like, do not accept them.

It's your brand. It's your business. You work with who want to work with and nobody else. Period. Life is too short to put up with the Satans of the world and their bullshit (sorry, Mom).

Get rid of trouble clients immediately. A better client will take their place. Even if you are desperate and need as much business as you can, it is still not worth it. A trouble client can kill your productivity, slow down your progress, and mess with your mindset. One message from a jerk will weigh heavier on your mind than 50 "we think you rock" messages will. Some clients just aren't worth the effort, and that's okay.

When I have a client who needs to be let go, I simply explain to them that my business is changing and I won't be able to serve their needs moving forward. I'm polite about it, and you should be as well. I also like to refer them to someone who can help them. I don't want to leave them in the cold. When possible, refer them to a competitor of yours, and let Satan become their problem.

Letting go of a client is never fun. It's not always easy. But the benefits far outweigh putting up with the hassle. Your productivity will increase because you will not be spending wasted hours on those bad clients. You maintain your momentum and energy. New sales will come. Better clients will replace them.

The best way to avoid ever having to fire a client is to attract the right ones to begin with. Your brand, once established, should attract people similar to you and who appreciate your values.

52

The Sound of Silence

THE SOUND OF SILENCE can be a dangerous thing in business. You work hard to build an engaging brand and enjoy the interaction between you and your target audience. So what do you do when your audience stops engaging with you and goes silent? You have to jump-start the conversation.

There are a few key areas in your business where you may have noticed them going quiet. You know your audience has gone quiet when you see a decrease in your e-mail open rates and click-through rates. A decrease in your retweets on Twitter and conversation/likes on Facebook. A decrease in blog comments, a decrease in referrals, and even a decrease in incoming phone calls. All of this can and will lead to a decrease in sales and opportunities.

Hopefully you'll only notice a decrease in just one of these areas. If that's the case, the fix is fairly easy. If every channel has gone quiet, then the first thing you need to do is check and see what you've done wrong. Any brand can screw up, especially personal brands. Sadly, I see a lot of people damaging their personal brand via social media on a daily basis. A strong opinion on something controversial can make your audience run the other way in a hurry.

Assuming you haven't massively screwed up, then fixing a silent audience can be quick and easy. Regardless of what company you use for handling your e-mail list, almost all of them provide statistics on open rates and click-through rates. You should monitor these and watch for trends and changes. If you see that your open rates have decreased, the first thing you should focus on is the subject line.

As I mentioned earlier in the book, the subject line of an e-mail is *the* most important part. It's the headline that determines whether or not your e-mail is going to get opened. You *must* write great subject lines. I spend more time working on the copy of the subject line than I do the e-mail itself—it's that important.

Your click-through rate is the number of times your subscribers click the links in your e-mail. One mistake I see marketers make frequently is including too many links in their e-mail. This drives me insane. Do you want them to click the link to your blog post or your Facebook profile? You can't have it both ways. Your readers are busy and aren't looking to go back and forth and check out every single resource you mention in the e-mail. Focus on one clear objective for each e-mail.

Also, *always* include a link in your e-mails. Never break this rule. Most people send out an e-mail filled with juicy content and helpful information—but no links. Then they send an e-mail a few days later with a fancy link to a sales offer. The problem? You're subconsciously training your readers to know that if they see a link, you're trying to get their money. So they stop clicking. But if every e-mail, even the ones that are 100 percent content, requires them to click a link to get to it, then you are training them to be in the habit of clicking your links.

Comments are the lifeblood of your blog. If they are few and far between or you've noticed they've dropped off from what they used to be, then there are a few things to fix. The first thing is to ensure that you are commenting back. It's an honor for someone to take the time to comment on what you've written. You owe it to them to comment back and engage them. Second, make sure you're writing blog posts that your audience wants. Give them what they need and keep on giving it to them. Blogging isn't about what you want to write about. It's about what your audience wants and needs.

The best way to keep conversation going on Facebook is to ask questions. People love to give their two cents on ... well, everything. Just like blog comments, you want to be sure to comment back to people. Engagement is a two-way conversation. You'll receive more interaction and Likes to your postings when it's relevant to your audience and, most importantly, when it's not boring. Nothing will kill the vibe of your community faster than being boring.

A drop off in retweets from Twitter is a super easy thing to fix. First, like your blog, put out great content. The content needs to be relevant to your target audience. Don't always quote someone. An original thought is far more likely to earn a retweet. Also, remember that the shelf life of an average tweet is next to nothing. This is why frequency becomes so important. You'll find that certain days and certain times of the day will bring you more retweets. But the key is to post a lot and post often.

Also, don't ask for a retweet unless it's for charity or some other good cause that is important to you. If your stuff is good, it will be shared. Asking for it seems desperate and is like asking for help before the person has received the value themselves. It's okay to encourage people to share, but trust your audience. They'll take care of you if you take care of them.

Something that frequently comes up when I'm consulting with a business is that they've seen a drop-off in referrals. My response is always, "What are people saying when you ask for them?" to which their response is almost always "Uh, we're supposed to ask for them?"

Yep, if you want more referrals start asking for them. It's amazing how simple business can be sometimes. There are three types of people: those who will always send you referrals whether you ask them or not (God bless these people!), those who will never send you a referral no matter what (screw 'em), and those who will—if you ask. No one wakes up and says, "I'm gonna see what I can do to help John's business today." (What a wonderful world we would live in if that were the case.) Give your customers an incredible experience and let them know you appreciate and expect their referrals. You'll be amazed at how effective this is.

You may also find a decrease in phone calls. This may actually be a good thing. I hate phone calls, and if I saw a decrease in them I'd be thrilled. Only very close friends and family know my cell phone number, and the truth is too many of them know it. Set up your communication channels the way you prefer to communicate. Most of my conversations are through e-mail, and then we take it to the phone when needed. I love phone calls when they are scheduled. Otherwise it's a distraction—or my mom wanting to know how my day was.

Consistency is a huge factor in engagement. If you don't go quiet on your audience, then they are less likely to go quiet on you. Communities love engagement, and yours is no different. Don't let your audience go quiet on you. It's not up to them; it's up to you. On a side note, if you have any tips on making a mother-in-law go quiet without going all "Dexter" on her, I'm open to suggestions.

53

The 10:100 Method

WOULD YOU RATHER HAVE A RAVING FAN or a satisfied customer? It is not a trick question. People are so focused on selling more, more, more that they never take a step back to evaluate if customers are happy or just satisfied. A happy customer is worth more than a satisfied customer. Too many businesses merely satisfy people rather than wow them. Happy customers are raving fans, and they should be getting your complete focus.

Raving fans are more loyal to your brand. They buy more of what you're selling more often. They spread the word about you. They become a strong brand advocate for you. Satisfied customers, in contrast, tend to keep their experience to themselves. Unlike your raving fans, your satisfied customers weren't so wowed that they have the desire or urge to share their experience with others.

Because most businesses are so focused on making as many sales as possible, they often overlook how customers feel when the purchase is over. Instead, the company quickly moves on to the next potential customer. This leads to what I call a churn-and-burn rhythm where businesses are always chasing the next sale.

There's no doubt your next sale is important, and you should know where it's going to come from. But when it comes to building a brand that lasts, don't get ahead of yourself.

The 10:100 method helps prevent you from getting too far ahead of yourself. Stop focusing on trying to convince millions of people to buy your product or service. Instead, shift your attention to the clients you have right now. Wow them. If you focus on 10 customers and absolutely rock their world, they will go out and tell hundreds. Too many businesses focus on the masses and neglect the opportunity sitting right in front of them.

There is nothing wrong with starting small. You just have to start. Gary Vaynerchuk has built an incredibly powerful and lucrative personal brand. Gary took his family's wine business from a few million dollars a year in revenue to well over $60 million in revenue. He did it by posting daily video wine reviews that were short, personable, and humorous. Gary took a traditionally stodgy industry (wine reviews) and turned it on its head. Rather than create dull, lifeless reviews like everyone else, he talked about wine tasting like feet or like Coke mixed with chocolate. He made wine approachable for the average person and ignored the millions of people who found his style offensive and lowbrow. In short, Gary focused on creating a few raving fans instead of just offering another "me too" wine review column.

At the height of his Wine Library TV show, Gary had over 90,000 daily viewers. But if you think he had thousands of people watching his videos from day one, think again. Gary started small—very small, in fact. He focused on the few people who were watching his show (about 5 to 10 people at first). He worked very hard to ensure they found the videos valuable and entertaining. He even used a chalkboard positioned behind him to write notes to his early followers and inside jokes that only they would get. He made them feel special and important because they were. He made them a part of his tribe. As a result, his early fans became loyal raving fans, and they eagerly shared Gary's videos with their friends. It snowballed from there. Before he knew it, Gary not only had hundreds, he had thousands of raving fans ready to buy anything he wanted to sell. He used the 10:100 method to launch his brand and business.

Casa Vieja is a nice little Mexican restaurant in my town that did not have a line at the door when they first opened. There's a ton of competition in the restaurant business, and there weren't a lot of marketing dollars put behind their opening. But the crew at Casa Vieja didn't let that stop them. When my wife and I would have lunch there, it was not uncommon to see only four or five other parties dining at any given time. Getting a table was never a challenge. Yet every time someone dined there they were greeted with great customer service and good food. They bring chips and salsa to your table immediately. The food always arrives at your table quickly, and they bring you to-go cups when you leave. They did a lot of little things that other restaurants overlook and created an unmatched dining experience. They focused on the tens of customers they had and made sure they were more than satisfied. Those early customers began spreading the word, and soon Casa Vieja had hundreds of customers. Today, they are almost always packed during lunch and dinner. People have to park in an empty lot next door because the parking lot fills up so quickly.

Put yourself in the consumer's shoes. When you go see a movie, do you want to come away satisfied? Or do you want to love it so much you'll get it on DVD the day it's released in stores? We all want an experience that is more than just adequate. Focusing on the masses causes you to take your eye off opportunities that are sitting right in front of you. Think of your last 10 customers. Did you blow them away with awesomeness? Or did they leave simply feeling content? They shouldn't just feel satisfied when doing business with you. They should feel ecstatic. They should leave as a new fan of yours. That's how great brands grow: one customer at a time.

54

Your Online Presence

DO YOUR PROSPECTS KNOW YOU EXIST? If you don't have a strong online presence, then there is a darn good chance they do not. It's one thing to have a blog or fancy website; it's another thing completely to have a strong online presence. Never before has it been so easy to build a strong personal brand. The tools available today are incredible. However, many entrepreneurs still get stuck in the process of building their brand and developing their presence, especially online.

It's easy to assume that if you have a website, blog, decent search engine optimization, and a Facebook account that you have a strong online presence. All of these are great, but there's more to it than that. Just because you own a toolbox doesn't mean you can build a house.

You have to approach this from your audience's point of view.

Your online presence needs to clearly answer three questions: who you are, what you do, and who it is for. *You* may feel like your online presence is strong, but if your target audience isn't "getting it," then you have a *big* problem. Confused prospects never buy. Let me state that again for dramatic effect: confused prospects never buy! Never underestimate the importance of clarity.

> Your online presence isn't just seen; it's felt.

When was the last time you evaluated your online presence? Now's as good as time as any I'd say. ☺ Here are seven questions your audience is asking about your website. How you answer them will help determine if your online presence needs some help.

1. What's In It for Me? Every prospect is always asking this question. Your website needs to answer this quickly. A strong benefit-driven headline is a must. Let people know *why* they should care. Let them know what's in it for them. It seems obvious, but a lot of websites miss this and therefore are missing out on a lot of business.

2. How Will I Know This Is for Me? Your site has to speak directly to your target audience and your target audience *only*. Let people know they belong. If your audience consists of stay-at-home moms who cook, for example, then when mortgage brokers land on your site, they should immediately know it's not for them. Speak your audience's language and let them know they've found a home.

3. What Is It You Want Me to Know? Make it crystal clear what you're about and what message you're trying to get across. Maybe you've got a better way businesses can market themselves. Get your message across. Scream it, shout it, do whatever it takes. No one should ever leave your site not knowing what you're about.

4. What Do You Want Me to Do Next? A cardinal sin in marketing is failing to have a call to action. People are silently begging to be led. Be that leader and tell them what the next step is. It can be something simple like asking for people to leave a comment on your blog (something you should do at the end of this post by the way) or something like asking them to join your e-mail newsletter or check out a special offer you're running. Always, always, always include a call to action. Don't assume people will know what to do; tell them or show them.

5. How Can We Keep the Relationship Going? So you put out great content. Fantastic! Now what? Let people know how they can connect with you and allow them the opportunity to connect through multiple channels. They should know how to get on

your e-mail list and how to connect with you on Facebook, Twitter, LinkedIn, or YouTube. Keeping the relationship going is a must. Nurture it, protect it, and grow it. Never take your relationship with your audience for granted.

6. How Can I Tell My Friends About You? People love to share awesome stuff. Assuming you produce awesome stuff, you are going to want to share it. Make it easy for people to spread the word about you and what you do! Social media has made this super easy to do online, so make sure your content can be shared through the main social media channels. Even your e-mail should be easy to share. Sure, they can just Fwd it along, but do *they* know that?

7. How Can I Learn More? This one is a biggie (that's what she said; sorry, I couldn't resist). If you've done a good job creating awesome content, people are naturally going to want to learn more. Your target audience is passionate about your topic, or they wouldn't be your target audience. One blog post or article isn't gonna cut it. Let them know how and where they can learn more. Maybe it's additional blog posts on the topic, your e-mail newsletter, or your product/service. Maybe it's a live event. What it is isn't as important as letting them know where it is. Assume people are going to want to know more and point them in the right direction.

These questions are a good way to evaluate your online presence. A strong online presence is a must when it comes to building a strong personal brand. Go through all of your sites and make sure you are making things crystal clear for your audience. It will go a long way toward building the strength of your brand and enhancing your brand awareness.

55

Raise Your Standards

ONE OF THE MOST DEADLY MISTAKES you can make with your business is to get comfortable. Sadly, I see it all the time. At some point you become relaxed, complacent even, and then you stop raising your standards. Your effort loses its juice. Suddenly things that would not normally be accepted have become standard.

When this happens, your customers begin to expect less of you. Over time they lose the excitement they once had about doing business with you. A restaurant in the town I live in was once known more for its cleanliness than it was for its food. Any time someone mentioned the restaurant in conversation, you could guarantee a comment would be made about how nice they kept the place. The floor was always swept clean, rarely would you see dirty dishes that needed to be taken to the kitchen, and the bathroom floors were clean enough to sleep on. (Regardless of how clean they were, I would never recommend sleeping on a bathroom floor. That would drive my OCD brain crazy. I need hand sanitizer just thinking about it.)

Anyway, over time customers began to notice that sometimes there sat tables that needed to be bused. They noticed the staff dressed more relaxed. The standards were being lowered. Eventually the restaurant looked nothing like the place its loyal customers had come to know and love. It didn't take long for them to start dining somewhere else.

When you have success, it's easy to sit back and take it easy. But that comes at a price. Low standards equal low profits. It is impossible to innovate when you stop pushing. You get success under your belt, and fear kicks in. If it's working, why try something new? An attitude like that is dangerous. It is dangerous because somewhere out there you have a competitor working very hard on implementing new ideas.

Building a loyal fan base is phenomenal, but if you sit on your laurels you are playing with fire. It would be okay to get comfortable with where you are if your audience did as well. But people are always raising their standards. The marketplace is changing every day, so why aren't you? Never take the loyalty and attention of your fans and supporters for granted. It is not enough to earn it once. You must earn it over and over again.

Every time I hear someone say, "Good enough is good enough," I know that is someone I do not want to do business with. Imagine if a brain surgeon had a good enough is good enough approach to surgery! A lot of marketing teachers preach the importance of taking action and just getting something out there. They have the right idea, but it's misguided. Taking action is the key to success. You can't magically attract success. But you can't have low standards and expect success. Mediocrity will not cut it. This "something is better than nothing" attitude is killing the quality of many brands. Your customers deserve better. I think Jack White says it best in The White Stripes song "Blue Orchid" when he says, "Something better than nothing, it's giving up."

At what point does it become okay to stop striving for more? When you're dead. I don't mean to get morbid, but why would you ever want to stop improving and growing both yourself and your business? You should never stop learning and working on your skills. Every area of your business can be better. At no point does the importance of education decrease. Maintain high standards and never stop pushing to be better. There is always room for improvement.

56

Warning: You've Been Lied To

YOU'VE BEEN LIED TO. I'm sorry for that, but it wasn't me. You've been told for years that there's no such thing as an overnight success and that sometimes in business you have to pay your dues first. That is not completely true.

Most of the people who say those things and think that way are slow. They are slow to take action. They are slow to implement. They are slow to make money. They are slow to reach success. That's not how you want to be, and that is not how you should be.

I have certainly paid my dues. I have experienced years of setbacks, mistakes, failures, embarrassment, and even shame. I have also experienced incredible success. But I never sat around waiting. I never took on a "these things take time" kind of attitude. If you have that attitude, I suggest you start working immediately to get rid of it. It's poison.

So many entrepreneurs take things slow when building their brand and business. They have the "Rome wasn't built in a day" philosophy. I get what they are saying, but remember that Rome *was* built. They completed it. They did not sit around wasting time thinking, "These things take time." They got off their butt and worked.

What's your attitude about time? How long will it take you to get your brand where you want it to be? The amount of time it takes to establish a solid brand in the marketplace is completely up to you. It can take a short time or it can take forever. It's your choice.

Are you writing off your lack of success as "paying your dues"? If you are, well then you are screwed. While you are paying those dues, the rest of us are making money, enjoying success, and living an awesome life. We aren't waiting.

Success doesn't have to take a long time. It doesn't have to take five years, ten years, or even one year. Get those thoughts out of your head. They are death to an entrepreneur.

I know of a real estate agent who experienced incredible success in a very short period of time. The average real estate agent sells about four to six homes per year. Not a lot by any stretch of the imagination. After a few years in the business they may be a "top producer" and sell 25 to 35 homes. Maybe. But Jim Striegel from Texas didn't want to wait.

In his first year in the business, Jim sold almost 200 homes. You read that right, 200. Most agents never sell 200 in their entire career, much less a single year. I once heard Jim speaking at a conference where he was asked the question we all have for him: how? How did he sell 200 in his first year in the business, with zero real estate experience, when it takes years for most to even hit 50 homes sold in a year?

Jim's answer was both simple and amazing. He said, "I didn't know it was supposed to take a long time." That is a very profound statement. Can you imagine if Jim bought into the idea of paying your dues? What if he focused on the fact that most agents sell four homes a year? I highly doubt he would have sold 20 homes, much less 200.

What are you buying into that is slowing you down? The largest brands in the world didn't get there overnight. But they also didn't take a lifetime to get there. Facebook and Google are two of the largest brands in the world. Neither one of them are even 15 years old.

> Success doesn't have to take forever. How long it takes truly is up to you.

I have attended a lot of conferences in my life. I am always shocked at the number of people who attend a conference and then don't do a thing when they get home. Often those that do have an elaborate plan of action for when they get home still don't implement anything they have learned. Here's my question for you: Why wait until you get home?

A friend of mine once learned an amazing new strategy at a conference. It motivated him to change all of his current advertising. We wrote the new ads during a break and then called back home to his local newspaper and told them he was faxing the new ads over. By the time the conference was over and he was back home, his new ads were published and he had fresh new leads sitting there waiting for him.

Why wait? Right now is always a good time to do something.

You may be just starting your business. You may be in debt from a past mistake. You may be struggling. I understand and sympathize with you. I really do. But please know that success is right around the corner. It is not hiding from you and it is not five years ahead of you waiting. It is right now. You can go from dead broke to $5,000, $30,000, $300,000 or whatever in 30 days. Maybe six months. Maybe three years. It is completely up to you.

Creating and building a brand and business that serves others and is successful isn't easy. It will take long hours, hard work, and busting your butt like you never have before. It will take you time. How much time it takes depends on your willingness to do the work required. Just remember that when you say you are paying your dues: who are you paying them to?

You can keep struggling and paying your dues. You can continue to assume these things take time. Or you can get fed up with that kind of attitude and start taking action toward your dreams. Success is now—if you want it.

57

Monitor and Measure

HOW CAN YOU IMPROVE YOUR BRAND if you don't monitor it and measure your visibility? The answer is that you simply can't.

You have to measure your reach, influence, visibility, and growth. You want to be sure all of your efforts are not going to waste. If you don't track and measure things, you can't complain when they don't improve.

There are numerous ways to measure your brand's success beyond just calculating incoming revenue. Pay attention to things like increases in your e-mail subscribers, social media following, website and video traffic, number of people contacting and interacting with you, and the number of opportunities presented to you.

Measuring your visibility and influence and knowing if you're doing well or not depends on your individual brand's goals and objectives. The quickest way to evaluate where you stand is to gauge how much interaction and feedback you get. When you blog, do you receive a lot of comments? Are you noticing new people commenting with each new post you publish? When you post something awesome on a social media channel, is it shared? Do people respond to it with questions or additional comments?

As you can see, there are many things to take into account with visibility and influence. There's more to it than just measuring the size of your e-mail list, Facebook fans, and website visitors. You always want to be sure your online following is growing.

Measuring your visibility has become much easier thanks to some wonderful tools, a lot of which are free. These are some of my favorite to use to measure your social media reach and influence:

Tweetstats.com, where you can find out how much you engage, who with, and how often you tweet.

SocialMention.com, where you can set up alerts of your brand, company, or competitor.

WebsiteGrader.com, where you can measure and track a number of elements about your website or blog.

Compete.com, where you can see how your site stacks up against the competition.

CrazyEgg.com, where you can see exactly how people interact and navigate with your website.

A number of additional resources are out there. Some of them are free, but take note that the ones that have a fee are usually worth it because they give you additional stats and insights. Possibly more than you'd ever want to know.

Brands often fear social media and blogs because they can't control what people say about them. I've got news for you: Brands never had control. People aren't talking any more now that we have the Internet and social media. It's just that now you can see what they are saying, whereas before you'd have to be standing right next to someone to hear what they had to say.

I often find that personal brands overlook the importance of monitoring their brand. Never assume that people are not talking about you. Even a small level of brand awareness will cause people to talk.

Every single day there is a conversation going on about your industry. If you decide not to participate in that conversation, you are digging your own grave. You want to make sure your brand positioning is strong in the marketplace. You want to know what is being said, and you want to pay attention to what is not being said.

With the right tools you can monitor your brand and analyze your position in the marketplace. You can know exactly what your customers think about what you are doing right and what you are doing wrong, as well as keep a close eye on your competition.

Setting up a Google alert at www.google.com/alerts is a great way to monitor your brand. You can set up an alert for your blog name, for example, and anytime someone mentions your blog online, Google will e-mail you with the link. You can also set up alerts for your company name, personal name, and competitor's names to see what's going on with them. The opportunities are endless.

Another great tool is www.twitter.com/search, where you can find out what conversations are going on about you, your market, or whatever on Twitter. Let's say you are in the squirrel-training niche. (I'm not sure if there are people out there who train squirrels, but if there are then they probably need some help.) You can use twitter.com/search to see what people are saying about their squirrels. Perhaps someone is looking for a better way to train their squirrel. You could be very helpful by pointing them in the right direction of course, or recommending a squirrel training guide. Obviously, I know very little about training squirrels, but you get the idea.

Monitoring your brand is about more than just customer service; it's about being helpful. When you help someone, you increase the odds of them buying from you dramatically. You get them in your corner.

Knowing what is being said about your brand is one thing. Listening and responding is another. This is where you take things to a whole new level. If something is said about you or your industry, then for the love of Pete, respond! There is nothing worse than a brand with no voice.

Beyond monitoring your brand stealthily, be proactive about it. Ask your clients, "If you could wave a magic wand and change one thing about us, what would it be?" Don't assume you know the answer. Their answers may surprise you.

Also, do not assume that customers will tell you when they have an issue with you. Most people are afraid to complain or voice concern. It's on you to create an environment where they feel comfortable enough to share their opinions. Let people know you value their thoughts. Your brand and your business will be better for it.

Never stop monitoring your brand or measuring your influence and reach. If you don't, then you can't expect to know what is working and what isn't. You can't make tweaks and adjustments because you don't know which areas need improvement.

58

How to Ensure Your Brand Fails

IT OCCURRED TO ME that I've done a lot of talking so far about how to make your brand awesome. Then it occurred to me that I'm leaving out all of you underachievers out there who don't like to be bothered with results. How do you know what to do? Well, you're in luck because here's your 10-step guide to making sure your brand is anything but successful.

Disclosure: These steps do not need to be completed in any particular order. Just doing a few of these will ensure your brand fails. Enjoy!

Step 1: Let fear keep you from taking action and trying new things. Doing something new is scary. Fear is your friend.

Step 2: Never ask anyone for help. They're likely wrong anyway, and you don't need them because you are always right.

Step 3: Think of every reason something will not work rather than every reason why it will.

Step 4: Constantly worry about what other people think. Constantly. Seriously, there is *nothing* more important than the opinions of others, especially those who you do not know.

Step 5: Only hang around negative people who like to complain. These are the people keeping it real.

Step 6: Understand you have to be lucky to succeed. Hard work is for employees, not entrepreneurs. You became your own boss so you wouldn't have to work.

Step 7: The very second you are faced with a challenge, quit.

Step 8: Let self-doubt rule your mind. Confidence is completely overrated anyway.

Step 9: Do everything in your power to fit in and be normal. Industry "norms" are norms for a reason. If everyone else is doing it, then it *must* be a good idea.

Step 10: Under no circumstance should you ever take action on your ideas. That idea might be successful, and then you'll have to work.

Bonus step: Within the first 10 seconds of meeting someone for the first time, try to sell them something. It makes them happy and shows that you really care about them.

59

What Is Killing Entrepreneurs?

THERE'S A LOT TO DO in building and maintaining a successful brand. As you go along this path, you're going to want to be sure you're focused on the right tasks and you are getting things done. Let's be sure you're set up for success. You want to create an environment and schedule that allows you to be super productive.

It has been said that multitasking actually lowers your IQ more than smoking marijuana. I'm not sure who did the research on this study, but I'm sure they had a good time. I know people who actually brag about their ability to multitask. Multitasking is not very efficient. Focus on one thing and one thing only. You'll be more productive and more efficient, and as a result you'll be able to consistently implement and follow through on your branding campaign.

Earlier I mentioned how distractions and interruptions are going to be the death of entrepreneurs. Every day you allow interruptions is a day closer to you being out of business. You have to stop allowing yourself to be distracted. When you get interrupted, it takes your mind almost 20 minutes to get back to where you were when you were distracted. This means if you're interrupted five times a day by an unscheduled phone call, e-mail, or whatever, that you are wasting about a hundred minutes every day. And I'm going to guess you allow yourself to be interrupted more than five times per day.

Make a list of everything and anyone that interrupts you or distracts you on a consistent basis. Put them in order starting with the worst and moving down to the not so bad. Then create a plan to eliminate the top three. Your productivity will increase immediately.

Also, make a list of the three biggest activities that generate the most results for your business and schedule them every day. Spend an hour on each one. This ensures that you don't fall out of a rhythm when promoting your brand. You'll blog more consistently, stay active in social media, and develop a nice routine for creating content and staying in touch with your target audience. Otherwise you'll end up spending three hours on social media one day and forgetting about it for the next five days. You'll publish a video with great content one month and then go the next three months without doing it again.

If you are going to manage your promotions and your brand successfully, then you are going to have to learn to manage your daily activities successfully. Every day you should know exactly which elements of your brand campaign you'll be focusing on.

It takes a great deal of patience and an incredible amount of determination to create and manage a successful brand. You have to stay on the right path consistently and do the things that need to be done. Create a routine and an environment that sets you up for success. Do something every day that grows your brand and strengthens the relationship you have with your target audience.

60

Twenty Rules

I KNOW, I KNOW. I hate rules too. Let's call them decrees instead of rules. It sounds more official that way. These 20 decrees are the core of how I run my business. They've come together after years of experience and consulting with successful brands across the world. You may not use all 20 in your business. Some of them may not be right for you. Take the ones that you resonate with and go with it.

1. **Fail faster than the competition.** If you're failing more often than your competition, it means you're taking action quicker than they are. In business, speed wins. Life is too short to wait for everything to be perfect.
2. **Celebrate your victories.** Isn't it funny how when something bad happens we spend all of our energy on it, yet when we have a success, even a tiny one, we just smile and keep moving forward? Stop putting all of your thought and energy into the failures. Celebrate every victory no matter how big or small. Reward the right behavior.
3. **Make it easy for people to buy.** Seriously, how hard is this? I was making an online purchase once from a site that made me fill out all of my information over the course of three different forms only to *then* tell me I needed to set up a username and

password first. People are trying to give you money. Don't make them jump through hoops to do it.

4. **Know what is working and what isn't.** Measuring and tracking things are not fun. But if you don't know what's working and what isn't, then you keep doing this failing forward stuff over and over without making any progress.

5. **It has to be ridiculously fun.** If something isn't fun, I just don't do it. Sometimes this drives my wife crazy because I've yet to find taking out the trash fun. I want my business to be fun, and I want the people doing business with me to have fun! When presented with an opportunity, my first test on whether or not I'll say yes to it depends on if it will be any fun.

6. **Customers have to "get" an idea right away.** If you're like me, you're never short on ideas. Ideas are great, but if it doesn't make sense to the customer, then it doesn't matter how great it is. I once heard a CEO tell his staff that a big idea they had tried that failed only failed because their customers weren't ready for it yet. Duh! That's like saying, "My hand is burning because I stuck it in fire." Obviously your "big" ideas have to be something your customers understand right away.

7. **Fire your most annoying customers.** You've already read an entire chapter on this, so there's not much else to say. Don't think about it; just do it.

8. **A reason why is a must.** If you don't have a good reason a customer should do business with you, then you should pack it up and call it a day. Just because you decided to start your own business doesn't mean they should use you. There has to be a reason why. Always.

9. **Deliver exponentially more value for the price.** If your product or service costs $500 then you want to deliver $5,000 worth of value. You can't overdeliver in terms of value. The last thing in the world you want to hear a customer say is, "I got my money's worth." They should get their money's worth and then some.

10. **Industry norms do not define you.** You make the rules. Don't fall into a trap of following the pack. In my opinion too many businesses are in the habit of riding trends. Don't sit and watch trends. Do something and cause trends.

11. **Ignore the minutia.** It's so easy to get caught up in trivial tasks and activities. Stop it. Always focus your time on the activities that will make you the most money. If it's not a high-dollar activity, then it's not the best use of your time. Delegate and outsource all of the things that can easily be done by someone else. If you want to make a high six- or seven-figure income, you can't spend time doing things you could pay someone $10 an hour to do.

12. **Generating leads is your business.** Leads are like oxygen. Without them your business will die a slow and painful death. Lead generation is always priority number one. It's not something you can put off until tomorrow. Every day you don't generate new leads is a day you weren't in business. It pains me to see so many entrepreneurs spending most of their time on things other than lead generation. Every successful business I've ever been in contact with consistently generates new leads.

13. **Have one more thing to sell.** I once held a paid seminar that was 100 percent content with no intention of selling the audience anything else. By the middle of the day we had people asking our staff if I provided coaching or consulting or something. They were looking for that next step. Your audience is looking for that next step. Make sure you have one to sell them.

14. **Personality is everything.** You've already got the gist of this by now unless for some strange reason you started reading this chapter first, which would be quite odd. Your business needs to have some personality, and it needs to be present in everything you do.

15. **Don't stop selling to your customers.** If someone makes a purchase from you once, they become way easier to sell a second time, assuming your product or service doesn't suck. Don't assume that just because they've purchased once they're done. Barnes & Noble sent me a coupon once that came just seven days after I had been in the store making a purchase. I went back and used the coupon the same day I received it.

16. **Do the opposite of your competitors.** It's okay to be the different one in your industry. "Normal" has been done already.

17. **Charge what you're worth.** Some businesses price themselves out of existence. If your prices are too low, you can't maintain your business. If they are too low, then you can't create a lot of value for your customers and you sure as heck can't provide them with an extraordinary experience. You deserve to be paid in accordance with the value you bring to the marketplace.

18. **Get help.** I'm not so egotistical to think that I have all of the right answers. I ask questions *all* of the time and constantly strive to learn from those much smarter than me. Being in a quality mastermind group is a must. Accountability keeps you moving and helps you stay on track. You can't build a winning brand all by yourself. Don't be too proud to ask someone for help. Also, don't be a jerk when someone reaches out to you for help.

19. **Always have a call to action.** People are begging to be led. You have to tell them and show them exactly what you want them to do. I've received a direct mail piece before from a company that didn't include a phone number, website, address, or any way to get in contact with them. I bet they are sitting there today complaining that direct mail doesn't work because no one called them.

     Traditional branding has no call to action. It's just how many impressions can they get for their logo. I have no idea how many times I've walked into a room and forgot why I was there. How am I supposed to remember what I saw on a billboard?

     Having a call to action on your marketing is good, but the call to action has to be strong. "Sign up for my newsletter" sucks. There's nothing compelling about that. Make the offer about them, not you. What if instead it said something like "Sign up to receive 25 percent off your next purchase and receive a free video that reveals the secrets to _____." It's not perfect, but it has a specific benefit so the person knows what to expect.

20. **Big is the enemy.** Most businesses start small and get bigger as things progress (that's what she said). You want to keep your business small because small companies can remain flexible and are better positioned to adapt when need be. No one cheers for

Goliath; they cheer for David. Blockbuster was a huge brand with hundreds, if not thousands of physical locations across the United States. Then Netflix comes along and has no physical locations, no late fees, and steals Blockbuster's thunder. Blockbuster was in a position where they could not easily adjust and implement new changes.

Just because you keep things small doesn't mean you can't be super successful. Richard Branson credits much of Virgin's success to the fact that they keep each sector of their company as small as possible. The world moves at a fast pace. Your brand's ability to change and adjust quickly is a huge asset.

Again, feel free to apply these decrees in your own business if you find some that really resonate with you. Also, don't hesitate to make your own list or add to this one. If you make an awesome decree in your business, be sure to let me know. I'd love to hear it.

61

Parting Shot

For the record, this isn't the end. It is just the beginning. Where you go from here determines what the next year of your business will look like. Will you be well positioned as a brand that delivers value and a brand that people trust? Or will you be virtually unknown, still podding along looking for the next sale? It's not up to me; it's up to you. You've got to make it happen.

> Ideas not implemented are worthless.

The reason so many so-called gurus try to sell you a secret formula to success is because the one thing that really determines your success isn't sexy. It's action. Take action and get results. Stop taking action, and your success stops. I want to see you take massive action on what you've just learned. Now is the time to start.

A winning brand is recognized, respected, and has a loyal following. The world is full of people with a strong message to share trying to be that winning brand. They are using every tool at their disposal to sell it. The best tool you have is your brand. How you use it is up to you.

Your success depends on people knowing what you do, why you do it, and how it adds value to their life; people who know your brand's story and see it in action as they engage with you on a regular basis. The relationships are meaningful to both parties. They are predisposed to do business with you and send business your way not because they know, like, and trust you but because you know, like, and trust each other.

> You win by delivering more value than anyone else.

It's up to entrepreneurs to keep the world going. We take risks. We take action. We make things happen. The world needs a brand like you, one that fights how things are normally done in an attempt to provide real value to your audience.

The tools and resources needed to build and promote your brand are more abundant than ever before. There is no excuse not to give it your all. Every action you take builds your brand. Enjoy the moment and the journey. Tomorrow is going to be awesome.

This isn't the end of the road for you and me. Send an e-mail to outcasts@brandagainstthemachine.com and subscribe to my special book owner list where you'll receive bonus sections, examples of people branding against the machine, and videos of me ranting about businesses that are doing it wrong. You'll also get access to private webinars and Q&A sessions as well.

With this parting shot I want to leave with you with a warning: **The machine isn't going to stop.**

Businesses will continue to force their message on the consumer by interrupting them constantly. Businesses will continue to compete on price rather than value, and they will continue to fall in line with how everyone else is doing it.

You have to break out of what is normal. Stop being ordinary. Be creative, be different, and be remarkable. Take a look at what normal is and do the opposite. Do what isn't supposed to be done.

I dare you.

Special Offer

Acknowledgments

NO ONE GETS ANYWHERE WITHOUT HELP. God has blessed me by putting some amazing people in my life who have helped me along the way. Undoubtedly I will leave someone out. If that's you, I'm truly sorry I forgot. You should've created a brand that stands out. ☺

These are the awesome people who have supported, encouraged, helped, influenced, and inspired me along my journey. I am eternally grateful to each and every one of you.

To Scott Stratten, your confidence in me is the reason this book exists. Your advice and assistance during this process were invaluable. Although your support has been amazing, it's our friendship that I am most thankful for. Thank you for having my back and being my golf caddie. You rock!

To Shannon Vargo, my editor at John Wiley & Sons, I still don't know how a 15-minute conversation got me a book deal, but I'm not questioning it. Your desire and vision of how we would make this book different was inspiring and refreshing. Thank you and everyone at Wiley for letting me stand out and for going against the "normal." And thanks to Elana Schulman, editorial assistant, for making life so easy on me during this entire process.

To Spencer Shaw, who has had my back more than anyone in the business. You've always been a phone call or text away whenever I needed something. Always. It's nice knowing there's someone else out there as crazy as me. Thanks for always calling me out when I needed it and for building me up when I needed that. You are a rock star, my friend.

To Craig Proctor, attending your conference for the first time changed my life and set me on the course that led me here. I've learned a lifetime of knowledge from you and probably wouldn't be an entrepreneur today had I not stumbled across your teachings. You continue to inspire me and influence me. You are a legend.

To Danny Griffin, for giving me the time of day when I was nobody. You've always been there whenever I needed help, and that means the world to me. We've had a long journey together, and I know the world hasn't seen anything yet!

To these amazing entrepreneurs I've learned so much from, you are the ones who set the standard for everyone else: Tony Robbins, Dan Kennedy, and Seth Godin.

To Ryan Lee, for playing a huge role in my business without even knowing it. Your approach to business became the model for everything I do. Thank you for that.

To Brian Moses, for inspiring me to set seemingly unreachable goals and then showing me how to reach them.

To Travis Robertson, your friendship and support in business, life, and with this book are appreciated more than you know. It came at a time in writing this book when I needed a push, and you provided that. You never let me settle and always push me to do a little better. I love that.

To Dean Hunt, for an exciting journey that led us both to so many new places. Thanks for the laughs and for reminding me how fun business can be if we make it fun. There aren't many people I would Zorb with, but you will always be one of them.

To my fellow entrepreneurs, who have made this world so much fun and have always supported me: Joey Strawn, Suzanne Gerety, Kyle Battis, Rory Stern, Joel Widmer, Felicia Slattery, Aaron Foster, Terry Wygal, Jason Elkins, James McDonald, Jason Pitre, Frank DeMarinis, Matt Shreves, Doug Krull, Bill Templeton, James Reynolds, Kristi Frank, Dan Russell, and John Giammarco.

To Dr. Mollie Marti: While on a late-night flight home from speaking at your event, the idea for this book was born. I will never forget that.

To Carrie Wilkerson, Paul Evans, Perry Lawrence, and Mark Thompson. Our dinner at a Pizza Hut in Texas made me realize that I've never wanted to do what I do so much.

To my mother-in-law Marilyn, for providing me with an endless supply of jokes. Few people in this world are as good a sport as you.

To the four people who inspire me most: Howard Hughes, Walt Disney, Richard Branson, and Jack White. Your level of creativity, passion, and drive is something I aspire to achieve.

To every client I have ever had: each and every one of you has influenced me in some way. I'm grateful for the opportunity to serve you.

To all the readers of my blog and to my friends on Facebook and Twitter, you are all so awesome it's amazing. The conversations we've had and the laughs we've shared mean the world to me. I hope to meet you all in person one day—minus the creepy ones.

To my mom, who has never once thought my crazy ideas were crazy. You are an amazing mother and an incredible friend. Without your love and support, this book would not have happened. Also, for the record, I am truly sorry for hooking jumper cables to your arm while you were driving.

To my dad, who taught me how to work harder than anyone else and taught me that making people laugh is a brilliant business strategy. Growing up watching you run your business made me never want to do anything else other than be my own boss.

To my brother Jason: Your being so freakishly talented at everything caused me to always tackle the impossible just to keep up with you. Without that push I wouldn't be here today.

To my Lord and Savior, Jesus Christ, for giving me a passion and a purpose to serve others.

To my wife and best friend Brooke—where do I begin? Your support has been legendary. You've made me who I am, and you are always there for me. Thank you for not only encouraging me on this journey but for being a part of it.

And last, but certainly not least, to my wonderful children Jack and Ava, thank you for your smiles.

Index

208